# LIFE, LOVE, LOX

## REAL-WORLD ADVICE
## FOR THE MODERN JEWISH GIRL

### CARIN DAVIS

RUNNING PRESS
PHILADELPHIA · LONDON

Library of Congress Control Number: 2009929924

ISBN 978-0-7624-3787-0

Cover photo by Steve Legato
Author photo by Tracy Birdsell

Cover and interior design by Joshua McDonnell
Edited by Kristen Green Wiewora
Typography: Akzidenz Grotesk and Bembo

Running Press Book Publishers
2300 Chestnut Street
Philadelphia, PA 19103-4371

Visit us on the web!
www.runningpress.com

# CONTENTS

**4**    CHAPTER 1:
KEEP 'EM SEPARATED (KEEPING KOSHER)

**18**    CHAPTER 2:
LOX, STOCK, AND BAGEL (LIFE-CYCLE EVENTS)

**36**    CHAPTER 3:
SHUL HOUSE ROCK (SYNAGOGUE)

**54**    CHAPTER 4:
TOO COOL FOR SHUL (COMMUNITY INVOLVEMENT)

**68**    CHAPTER 5:
PUT A LID ON IT (HEADCOVERINGS)

**80**    CHAPTER 6:
ARE YOU MY MENSCH? (DATING)

**96**    CHAPTER 7:
FRIDAY NIGHT LIGHTS (SHABBAT)

**111**    CHAPTER 8:
HAPPY JEW YEAR (ROSH HASHANAH)

**127**    CHAPTER 9:
NAUGHTY JEWISH SHUL GIRL (YOM KIPPUR)

**140**    CHAPTER 10:
THE FESTIVAL OF LIGHTS. AND PRESENTS (CHANUKAH)

**152**    CHAPTER 11:
LITTLE MISS SHUSHAN (PURIM)

**167**    CHAPTER 12:
HOW TO LOSE A GUY IN TEN PLAGUES (PASSOVER)

**184**    CHAPTER 13:
CHALLAPALOOZA (OTHER HOLIDAYS)

**202**    HEEBONICS GLOSSARY

# CHAPTER 1

# KEEP 'EM SEPARATED
## (KEEPING KOSHER)

I'm a lifelong ham-dodger. I'm a clam-basher, a crab-evader, an anti-shrimpest. I pass up pepperoni, I just say no to bacon, and I sidestep soft-shell crab. I am the few, the proud, the Kosher.

I can't say the same for most of the men I date. Jewish? Always. Kosher? Rarely. To them, a hamburger without cheese is like Sheket Bevakasha without the "hey." So while keeping kosher enhances my spiritual life, it complicates my dating life.

Take my relationship with Jeff, a quick-witted movie exec who had me at "Shalom." Actually, he had me when his taut tuchus walked through my neighbor's front door, but the "Shalom" shout-out didn't hurt.

On our first date, he took me to a downtown diner that serves upscale comfort food. I ordered truffle mac-and-cheese, he ordered Mama's famous meat-loaf, and we split a bottle of syrah I was secretly happy he could swing. Between the good food, the great company, and my slight buzz, our dinner blinked by. As I enjoyed my last morsel of cheesy perfection, Jeff took a bite of meatloaf, slid my way, and stole a kiss. Or at least he started to until I ducked. Yes, ducked. No, I'm not a big tease, I'm a big Jew, and technically a mid-bite kiss would have meant mixing milk and meat. When Jeff's mouth touched mine, I didn't see fireworks, I didn't hear wedding bells: I heard the great rab-bis reminding me not to seethe a calf in its mother's milk.

I tried not to panic, but the whole date had gone to trayf, and I needed to fix it fast. The Talmud doesn't teach us how to apply kashrut laws to kissing; but since I ate dairy and Jeff ate meat, I could have used the milk-before-meat rule, where you wait thirty minutes, eat something pareve, and then gargle. Although I doubt gargling was the deep-throat action Jeff was hoping to see that night. Now, some rabbis say if a dairy knife is accidentally used to cut cold meat, it should be thrust into the dirt ten times. So perhaps I should have stuffed my mouth with soil; I'm sure that would've impressed Jeff—I hear men like it when women talk dirty. I could have just been honest with Jeff and explained why I wasn't in the mood for making out. Not tonight, honey, I had dairy.

I know I could have avoided this whole mishegas by being upfront when we first placed our order, but I don't feel comfortable recruiting my first dates for active kosher duty. I can't tell a man I just met what he can and can't eat for dinner. There are three little words a woman should never say too early in a relationship: "He'll have the . . ."

So when should we have "The Talk"? After a week? A month? A year? At what point should I let a man know that saying yes to me means saying no to other women—and to other meats? Keeping kosher is one of my dealbreakers, so eventually Jeff would have to ditch his little black recipe book and sever ties with all his ex grill-friends. He can't have his milk and eat meat, too.

"Can I have a man cave in the basement where I cook cheeseburgers on a George Foreman?" Jeff asked during one of our kosher coupling chats.

That would render the whole house trayf. And be a fire hazard.

"Can I rent a separate apartment just to cook nonkosher meals?"

I suppose he could keep a small place on the side for all his afternoon delights—or in this case, afternoon snacks. But I don't think I could handle that kind of open relationship. If a man commits to me, he commits to my kitchen. It's all or nothing, ko-way or no way. Keeping kosher is how I connect to Judaism every day in a concrete way, and I want to share that connection with my spouse. I want the Jewish American dream: a loving husband, 2.5 children, and two sets of dishes.

"Well, if you buy two sets of dishes, can I buy two sets of golf clubs?"

By Moses, I think he's got it! I don't see why he can't keep separate golf carts or own two game systems or play in two fantasy football leagues.

"What about two women?"

Don't push it, schmendrik.

A few weeks later, Jeff started whipping up kosher versions of his favorite trayf treats: chili cheese dogs topped with soy cheddar, pizza bagels loaded with veggie pepperoni, and barbeque chicken pizza with soy cheese and a pareve crust. I think he's getting the hang of it, maybe even enjoying it. And while I don't want to count my kosher chickens before they hatch, I wouldn't be surprised if ultimately Jeff and I end up sharing separate dishes but not separate bedrooms.

# BEEFING UP YOUR KOSHER KNOWLEDGE

During your *Of Mice and Mensch* dating adventures, you may meet up with a man who keeps kosher. Already down with kashrut? You're good to go. Never say no to pepperoni? Don't know your *milchig* (dairy) from your *fleishig* (meat)? Don't panic, just brush up on the basics.

The word *kosher* means "fit" or "proper." It not only applies to food but to kitchenware, Torahs, mezuzahs, tefillin, and tallit that are properly prepared and fit for use. People also throw it around in everyday phrases like "something's not kosher in Denmark." Not that the Danes are known for their blatant mixing of milk and meat.

At its core, keeping kosher isn't complicated, it just involves following a few strict food rules:

**NO MILK WITH MEAT.** Don't eat milchig and fleishig in the same meal, don't cook them in the same pan, and don't eat them with the same fork. When it comes to food, utensils, plates, pots, cutting boards, even sinks and sponges, you've got to keep 'em separated.

**GONE FISHIN'.** Seafood must have scales and gills, and can't be scavengers or bottom-dwellers. Forbidden foods include shrimp, lobster, crab, clams, calamari, eel, oyster, octopus, shark, and dolphin. Even swordfish and catfish are off the menu. But feel free to reel in salmon, trout, tuna, halibut, sole, and sea bass. Or just pick it up at the fish market if, like me, you haven't reeled anything in since vying for that Brownie merit badge in second grade.

**LAND ANIMALS MUST HAVE CLOVEN HOOFS AND CHEW THEIR CUD.** Cows and lamb are in; pigs and horses are out.

**IF YOU WANT TO AVOID FOWL PLAY, STAY AWAY FROM BIRDS OF PREY** (and the twenty-four other forbidden birds listed in the Torah), including hawks, ostriches, owls, and ravens. Feel free to serve up turkey, chicken, and duck with a clear conscience.

**PREDATORS ARE A NO-GO.** If an animal hunts other animals, we don't eat it. When was the last time you walked into a Jewish home and saw a mounted moose head above the fireplace? Exactly. Jews don't hunt; our food shouldn't either.

**IT'S NOT ENOUGH JUST TO MAKE THE LIST AT THE DOOR!** To get into the kosher club, animals must be killed mercifully and soaked and salted properly.

**EGGS FROM KOSHER ANIMALS ARE KOSHER, BUT BLOOD IS NOT.** If you see a red speck in your egg, toss it out. Out damned spot, out.

## A GOOD SIGN

If you're shopping at a kosher market, you can be confident everything you toss in your cart is good with God. But what should you do when you run to the corner store? Look for a hechsher. What the heck's a hechsher? A *hechsher* is a stamp of approval, a thumb's-up, the Jewish a-okay sign. It's an endorsement given by an established rabbinical authority that certifies a food or restaurant's kosher status. Think of the rabbinical council as the Godfather and the hechshered product as a made man.

Hechschers can be found on packaged foods, canned goods, and frozen items in grocery stores worldwide. In an effort to top the twelve tribes of Israel, there are now nearly 400 different rabbinical groups that offer hechsher services. Hechsher symbols often feature the letter K standing alone, inside a shape, beside a rabbinic council's initials, or incorporated into a Hebrew language seal. The Orthodox Union, the largest authority group, drops its OU tag on over 660,000 products, in over 5,000 facilities, in 77 countries. That's status.

The food tattoos don't end there. A hechsher is often immediately followed by the letter D or the letter P. The letter D indicates that the food is dairy and contains a milk product; P indicates that the food is pareve.

## STUCK IN THE MIDDLE

People who keep kosher are always tossing around the word *pareve*, which means "neutral." Pareve foods—like eggs, nuts, fish, fruit, grains, and vegetables—are the culinary khakis; they go with everything. They are neither milk nor meat and can be mixed with food in either column. Think of it this way: pareve foods swing both ways.

## POUR SOME SUGAR ON ME

Kashrut laws not only apply to food but also to beverages. Many juices, sodas, and wines wear a seal of approval. What makes wine kosher? Despite what you discovered from breaking into your parents' liquor cabinet and stealing swigs of Manischewitz, wine is not made kosher simply by making it sweet. That "one lump or two?" practice started in the early 1900s, when low-sugar Concord grapes were the only ones available to immigrant winemaking Jews. So they added sugar, and then a little more sugar, to help fermentation and balance out the wine.

Today, many vineyards around the world produce award-winning, high-end kosher wines that stand up to their nonkosher counterparts. Specialty wine stores, kosher grocers, and kosher wine Web sites carry hechshered vino from South Africa, Spain, Argentina, Chile, Australia, Italy, Israel, Napa, and dozens of other regions. Jews can actually make good wine? I'll drink to that! L'chaim!

Like food preparation, kosher winemaking has special laws. In short, no animal products can be used during filtering (non-K wines often use egg whites or gelatin), all ingredients used (like yeast) must be kosher, vines must be at least four years old, and only Shabbat-observant Jews can participate in the winemaking process. A flash-pasteurizing process called *meshuval* helps kosher wines get around this last one. Remember kosher wine gets you just as drunk as the nonkosher stuff; so chug away, fellow Jews, chug away.

## KOSHER COCKTAILS

Let's talk about Heebs and hard alcohol. Jews hold wine to strict standards because it's used in religious rituals, but we tend to be more lenient when it comes to our liquor and beer. Most assimilated Jews don't even look for a hechsher on the hard stuff, but observant Jews want all their booze approved by a higher authority. Why? Some beers and liquors are fermented with nonkosher yeast or contain blenders that are derived from nonkosher cream, wine, or glycerin. No matter how observant you are, don't get so drunk that you swallow the tequila worm—insects are always trayf.

## HOME IS WHERE THE HECHSHER IS

Modern Jews keep kosher to varying degrees, ranging from glatt kosher to kosher-style to a total no-go on the ko. There are more approaches to keeping kosher than there are colors in Joseph's coat. Here are a few of the more standard varieties:

- Some Jews keep kosher at home and will only eat out at certified kosher restaurants and other kosher homes.
- Some Jews keep kosher at home, but eat vegetarian or fish dishes out anywhere.
- Some Jews keep kosher at home, but eat nonhechshered meat out anywhere. They won't order a cheeseburger, but they'll devour a hamburger.
- Some Jews keep kosher at home, but order in from nonhechshered places and eat on paper plates with plastic silverware. They'll get pizza delivered, just not pepperoni.
- Some Jews don't keep kosher at home, but won't eat shellfish or pork products anywhere. Home or away.

## KOSHER COUPLING

What if only one person in a relationship keeps kosher? Don't let the bacon come between you. If your boyfriend is a ham-dodger and you're not, don't put him on the defensive. Show him you're willing to learn about his kosher way of life. Let him know you're open-minded and flexible . . . men like women who are flexible. Who knows, you may discover that saying "so long" to trayf is simple. And using separate dishes? It's no schvitz off your back.

Now, if you're the shrimp-shunner of the two, show your boyfriend that your kosher routine won't make dating difficult. Movies, parties, and concerts don't involve food, so you can still hit the town for the night. Many ballparks have kosher concession stands, and all have veggie options, so he can still take you out to the ballgame. You can order veggie dishes at mainstream restaurants, and most major cities, including New York, Chicago, Miami, Toronto, Philadelphia, and L.A., have kosher pizza, Chinese, Italian, burger, steak, and fish joints. So you can still go out to eat. And every city has bars. So you can still get piss-drunk, go back to his place, and play with his kosher salami.

# SHOULD YOU GO KO?

You've heard keeping kosher is a pain in the tuchus. That's all you need is one more source of *tsouris* (trouble) in your life. You barely have time to defrost a frozen entrée; who has time to cook a kosher meal? Well, good news, lazy Jews: no need to kick your microwave habit, there are plenty of kosher frozen entrées. And since many mainstream food companies (including Kraft, Keebler, ConAgra, General Mills, Tropicana, and more) have their products hechshered, your pantry may already be stocked with kosher goods.

Born to shop? Kosher grocers and butcher shops will have the widest kosher selection. But if you don't want to schlep to one, many grocery chains (like Kroger, Ralph's, Jewel, Albertson's, Vons, Publix, Shaws, ShopRite, and Winn-Dixie) and specialty food stores (like Whole Foods, Costco, and Trader Joe's) shelve kosher brands or have designated kosher aisles. Some carry prepackaged kosher meat from companies like Hebrew National, Empire, and Aaron's Best. Who knew you could grab kosher ground chuck while picking up a bottle of Two Buck Chuck?

## THE COST OF KEEPING KOSHER

You're living paycheck to paycheck; you have to cover your rent, your car, and your utilities. And your bar tab. And those new knee-high black boots you bought. So how can you afford to keep kosher? Isn't it expensive? It's true that kosher meat can cost more, but you're getting top quality. Who wants to eat subpar steak? And stocking up on a second set of kitchenware doesn't have to be spendy. A second set of silverware: $50. A second set of pots and pans: $100. A second set of dishes: $150. Getting in good with God: priceless.

## DO I LOOK LIKE I NEED TO GO ON A DIET?

With South Beach, Weight Watchers, and so many other fad diets, why are Jews still keeping kosher? Why should you keep kosher?

- Because I said so, that's why. The Torah doesn't give a reason behind keeping kosher; it just lays down the law.

- It's a simple daily act that reminds us of our Judaism—in the one place God knew Jews would see it. On our plates.

- Three thousand years of beautiful tradition, from Moses to Sandy Koufax. . . . Keeping kosher connects us to our Jewish ancestry. My parents, my grandparents, and all my crazy relatives since Mount Sinai have all been ham-dodgers. What, like I'm going to be the one to break that chain?

- It turns out what's good for the soul is good for the bod (It's worked well for my little size 2 number.) While kashrut wasn't necessarily created as a health code, kosher foods are held to a higher standard.

- Getting married? Keeping kosher is the perfect excuse to register for two sets of silver, china, bowls, pots, and pans. And what Jewish bride can say no to that?

# DINNER WITH THE KOSHER NOSTRA

After six months of dating your kosher boychik, he invites you to the suburbs to meet his *mishpacha* (family). Nothing fancy, just a casual dinner, a brief interrogation about your childbearing potential, and—oh yeah—his parents keep kosher. Don't worry—if their boy likes you, they'll like you. What's not to like?

So you talk too much, rarely go to shul, and are currently schtuping their son out of wedlock: they'll still think you're the best thing since sliced challah—as long as you don't mix their milchig dishes with their fleishig silverware. Here are a few pointers so you don't Focker things up:

**BYOB—BRING YOUR OWN BRIBE.** You don't want to be greeted with "Nu? She couldn't bring a little something?" It doesn't have to be expensive, just thoughtful. And kosher.

**IF YOU DON'T KNOW WHERE ON THE KOSHER-STYLE SPECTRUM** your hopefully future in-laws fall, assume they're as kosher as they come. Don't bring anything from the supermarket that doesn't have a hechsher. This stamp of approval lets you—and your host—know it's all good. Cookies, chocolates, cheese, salad dressing—it all needs the telltale tattoo. Bypass the bakery and deli counter; the food and equipment haven't been *kashered* (made kosher). And choose a whole fruit basket over a sliced fruit tray; what if the grocery store's deli knife sliced a ham before it cut the pineapple? Oy!

**IF YOU HEAD TO A BAKERY, MAKE SURE IT'S A KOSHER ONE.** How can you ID a kosher bakery in your hood? There will be a certificate on the wall that confirms its kosher status. Also, they're usually named something subtle like "Shlomo's Kosher Bakery." Be sure to ask if the bakery is dairy or pareve. You don't want to bring a cake that's kosher, but dairy, if his mama's making roast beef.

**REMEMBER TO SHOP EARLY;** kosher businesses are closed Friday nights and Saturdays for Shabbat. You'd hate to make a special trip for nothing. Sorry, folks, park's closed. . . .

**KEEP THE KOSHER SWEETS IN THE BOX WITH THE BAKERY'S NAME.** Like a Coach bag's signature C, it lets everyone know who made it. Not only will the designer label put his folks at ease, but they'll know you went through the extra effort. Parents give As for effort.

**WINE.** Hopefully you haven't been hitting the bottle so hard that you've already forgotten what you read in the kosher wine section (page 9). If you are that *farshikkert* (drunk) wait until you sober up to meet the folks. They won't want their son dating a lush, even if you're guzzling the kosher sauce.

**FLOWERS.** Everyone loves flowers. Tulips, sunflowers, Gerber daisies: you're good with any kind of foliage. Just skip the poinsettias, holly wreaths, and *schlocky* (cheaply made) grocery store bouquets. The first two are a little goyish, and the third is a little tacky. Actually, a lot tacky.

**KOSHER WINE, CANDY, AND SWEETS ARE SOLID**, but if you're celebrating a holiday, staying for the weekend, or gunning for Bubbe Malka's heirloom engagement ring, think outside the gift box. Bring a matzah tray for Passover, a bagel slicer for Break Fast, or a challah board for Shabbat. Bring something that says, I'm grateful for the invite, I'm happy to be here, and I'm way better than the last girl he brought home.

**WANT TO RIDE OFF INTO THE SUNSET?** Get to his parents' before sunset. Shabbat and Jewish holidays start at sundown, so leave work early and arrive on time.

**OFFER TO HELP IN THE KITCHEN, BUT STOP AND ASK FOR DIRECTIONS FIRST.** Find out which drawer holds the right silverware and which cabinet has the proper plates. The last thing you want to do is serve his mom's award-winning brisket on her favorite milchig platter. It's the culinary equivalent of pairing your brown Steve Madden platforms with your black Armani dress—total mismatch.

**GOT MILK? DON'T ASK.** If something's not on the table, it's probably not supposed to be.

**YES, YOU'VE GOT A GREAT RACK AND A TIGHT TUSH. SAVE IT FOR THEIR SON.** You want to look pretty, classy, and like you have no personal knowledge of how their son's bris went.

**DON'T PLAY WITH HIS MATZAH BALLS UNDER THE TABLE.**

# PAREVE MANDELBROT

Ladies and Gentlemen, tonight's closing act will be my family's world famous *mandelbrot* (almond bread). Think of them as my bubbe's biscotti. An outstanding pareve dessert, these versatile cookies have costarred opposite milk and have appeared onstage after meat. They're also perfect for dunking in your morning coffee or sneaking as a midnight snack. They're easy, traditional, and impressive. Thou shall not serve bland pareve desserts again.

## COOKIES

½ CUP VEGETABLE OR CANOLA OIL

1 CUP SUGAR

3 EGGS

3 CUPS ALL-PURPOSE FLOUR

1 TEASPOON BAKING POWDER

¼ TEASPOON BAKING SODA

1 TEASPOON VANILLA EXTRACT

1 CUP SLICED ALMONDS, CRUSHED

2 CUPS PAREVE SEMISWEET OR DARK CHOCOLATE CHIPS (OPTIONAL)

## TOPPING

5 TABLESPOONS GRANULATED SUGAR

1 TABLESPOON CINNAMON (OR TO TASTE)

Preheat oven to 350°F.

Mix the oil, sugar, eggs, flour, baking powder, baking soda, and vanilla together by hand. Add almonds and chocolate chips, if using, until thoroughly combined.

Mix the sugar and cinnamon for the topping together until thoroughly combined. Set aside.

Roll the batter into two (12-inch) logs (about the size of a sub sandwich before you throw out the bun to avoid eating the carbs). Sprinkle with cinnamon and sugar topping to taste, reserving some.

Place the logs on a cookie sheet. Bake for about 20 to 25 minutes. Catch up on your TiVo while waiting.

Remove from oven. While still warm, cut the logs into ¾-inch slices. Like you, the cookies want an even tan. So turn each slice on its side, sprinkle with remaining cinnamon-sugar, and bake for an additional 10 to 15 minutes, or until sides are lightly toasted. Since you're double-baking, keep an eye on the cookies, so they don't get *farbrent* (burnt).

Let cool. Smile and gloat as guests kvell about your baking.

**TIPS:**

- Pareve chocolate chips can be found at Trader Joe's and kosher groceries.
- I know I said the chocolate chips were optional, but really, when is chocolate ever a bad choice? Can I get an Amen?
- Torn between chocolate chip and plain? Split the batter into two. Add 1 cup chocolate chips to one half, leave the other half bare. Roll both into logs, and sprinkle with cinnamon and sugar. Who said you can't have it both ways?
- To step up the sweetness, I skip the sprinkle of cinnamon and sugar, and pour the cinnamon and sugar topping onto a piece of waxed paper and roll the log through it, so the mandelbrot is covered on all sides.

# CHAPTER 2

# LOX, STOCK, AND BAGEL
## (LIFE CYCLE EVENTS)

I don't have time to stop and talk. Walk with me while I write. I'm totally swamped. I have a ton of things to do. I haven't heard back from the party planner. I haven't decided on the dress. Or the menu. Or the flowers. And apparently the sterling-silver grapefruit spoons I registered for have been discontinued, and I obviously can't live without those. So now I have to run to Macy's to pick out a new pattern. What? Oh, no, I'm not getting married . . . I'm getting Bat Mitzvahed.

Well, re-Bat Mitzvahed. I had my big day at B'nai Tikvah when I was twelve. But like couples who renew their wedding vows, this time I mean it. I want to be active in the Jewish community. I want to be a leader. I want to get involved. Actually, I want the gifts. And the party. And the photo album. I'm ready for my close-up. And I'm tired of waiting for Mr. DeMille, or Mr. Stein, or whatever my husband's name will be.

Besides, Bat Mitzvahs are wasted on the young. When I was in junior high, I attended at least one Bar or Bat Mitzvah a weekend. I got all faputzed, ate tons of free food, and champagne-snowballed with lots of single Jewboys. But who appreciates an eight-piece band, an open bar, and dancing with unmarried men at that age? That's why an adult Bat Mitzvah is genius. This time around my friends and I will relish every minute of it. Plus, my competitive limbo skills have totally improved since then.

I know, I know, now we have weddings for that sort of thing. But not my wedding; I'm single. I'm not getting married anytime soon—and I'm fed up with waiting for Caphalon.

Don't I deserve nonstick? I don't mean to kvetch, but while my friends are all eating off fine china, sleeping on high thread count, and lighting sterling Shabbat candlesticks—that I bought them—I'm eating off mismatched plates, sleeping on T-shirt sheets, and saying the blessings over Glade vanilla-scented candles. I can't afford to buy myself the things I've bought my friends. How farkakt is that?

I don't care about always being a bridesmaid; I care about always being bridesmaid broke. I've schlepped to bridal showers, bachelorette weekends, and destination weddings. I've spent cash on countless engagement gifts, cocktail dresses, and airline tickets. And now I expect my friends to treat my second Bat Mitzvah with the same excitement and hoopla as I treat their weddings.

My Bat-smaids can start by throwing me an engagement party. Don't roll your eyes at me. I'm engaging myself to God. That's not worth a shindig? He's way better than some of the nuchschlepers my friends got hitched to. Then I want a shower with finger sandwiches, petits fours, and oh-so-fascinating party games like guess how many kippot are in this jar. And they are so totally planning me a wild Bat-chelorette party in Vegas. Ladies, let the dice and the good times roll.

I know it sounds like a meshuggene plan. But good men are harder to find than the afikomen. So rather than wait for a proposal, I'm proposing a second Bat. It's not that odd. It's like a wedding—if my fiancé were Elijah. There'll be a rabbi-led ceremony, Hora-dancing, wine-drinking, and people shouting "Mazel Tov!" I'll have a party with centerpieces, place cards, and a guest book.

I'll have a sweets table. I'll have a first dance. I'll be hoisted up in a chair. I'll have it all—lox, stock, and bagel. The only thing missing will be the man. For now. Someday my mensch will come. I know he will. I'm sure he will. But until then, you can find my re-Bat Mitzvah registry at Macy's, Crate and Barrel, and Bed Bath and Beyond. And please, no Israeli bonds or $18 checks.

# SUNRISE—LET'S EAT. SUNSET—LET'S EAT.

Okay, fine, re-Bat Mitzvahs probably won't replace weddings any time soon, so for now single girls like me will have to settle for celebrating other people's *simchas* (joyous occasions). And there are plenty of those Jew food-filled celebrations to enjoy. Jews love to rejoice with food, and we'll eat at the drop of a kippah. Someone tied the knot? Let's eat. Someone became a man? Let's eat. Someone got their schmekel sheared? Let's eat. Not only do Jews like to eat at life-cycle celebrations; God actually commands us to. We're obligated to enjoy a *Seudat Mitzvah* (festive meal) after we fulfill a mitzvah. Who's going to argue with that? Besides Jenny Craig. There are four major life-cycle mitzvahs that are followed by a mandatory meal: a brit milah, a Bar or Bat Mitzvah, a wedding, and a shiva. You could play arm candy at all of them, so let's brush up on the details.

**EVENT: BRIT MILAH (COVENANT OF CIRCUMCISION)**
**DESCRIPTION: A COMING-OFF PARTY**
**STARRING: A NEWBORN BABY BOY**
**SIGNIFICANCE: TO UPHOLD ABRAHAM'S COVENANT WITH GOD**

Your boyfriend just became an uncle; he has a new nephew Jake. If you're hoping to become Jake's aunt someday, you better be at his bris this week.

The Torah commands that all Jewish boys have a brit milah (or "bris," as the kids say these days). This slice-of-life ritual is a renewal of the covenant made between God and Abraham. It's a connection to past generations. It's a permanent symbol of Judaism in the one place a man won't miss it. That's right: God left a Post-it note on his penis. Hi, Son, please think twice before sleeping with a shiksa. Love, your almighty Father.

The bris itself breaks down into three quick parts:

- **Blessings and the big cut**
- **Kiddush and the baby naming**
- **Blessings and we eat**

While it's not necessary to have a *minyan* (quorum of ten Jewish adults) present, there's usually a packed house. A bris is a simcha that new parents want to share with all their friends and family. They also want to show off how happy their strapping young son will make the Jewish ladies someday.

Technically, the father is responsible for performing the bris, but Jews don't do "do-it-yourself." When was the last time you saw your dad use a tool? Forks don't count. We call a plumber to fix the pipes, a landscaper to cut the lawn, and a mohel to cut our son. The mohel is an observant Jew who knows how to medically, ritually, and very carefully perform a bris. He's a professional Clipper. Like the NBA team, but hopefully with better aim.

The boy's parents want the mohel to keep two hands on the wheel, so they pass out ceremonial honors to three lucky friends. The *kavatterin* brings the baby into the room, the *kvatter* gives the baby to the mohel, and the *sandek* holds the baby during the big snip. I think my last date's sandek let him squirm too much. To limit the squirming and reduce the pain, the baby is given a little wine before the ceremony starts. Compared to the taste of the Manischewitz Cherry, the pain of circumcision is nothing.

After the ceremony is complete, the guests get their nosh on. There's no prescribed bris menu, but you're usually looking at lox, bagels, smoked fish, herring, and tons of dessert. Yes, this poor boy just had his privates hemmed, and the guests are debating if they want an egg bagel or an onion bialy; but the meal is a commanded Seudat Mitzvah. Plus the circumcision itself makes everyone think of those handy-dandy bagel slicers.

## When, where, wear:

The bris occurs on the boy's eight-day birthday. Rain or shine, Shabbat or holiday, that's when the mohel's taking a little off the top. The only way for the baby to get out of it is to call in sick. Even then, the bris is just postponed; there'll be a makeup test waiting for him when he returns. To top it, the bris typically takes place in the AM. "Good morning, this is the front knife with your wake-up call."

The bris is held at either the parents' house or the synagogue, so don't come looking like a zhlub. Wear a nice wrap dress, your go-to Banana Republic skirt, or a funky jacket, jeans, and heels combo.

## What to bring:

It's not necessary to bring a gift, but giving one will score bonus points with your boyfriend's brother and sister-in-law. In other words, go directly to Baby Gap. Do not pass go, do not spend $200. Around $30 is good.

...................................................................................................

**EVENT: BAR/BAT MITZVAH (SON/DAUGHTER OF COMMANDMENT)**
**DESCRIPTION: A COMING-OF-AGE**
**STARRING: AN AWKWARD TWEEN**
**SIGNIFICANCE: TO CELEBRATE THE TRANSITION INTO ADULTHOOD**

Your boyfriend asked you to be his date to his second-cousin Maddie's Bat Mitzvah. It might not be bling, but it's a big step. Bat Mitzvahs are a big deal. A girl comes of age, her relatives come to town, and her dream boy comes to her party. It's like a John Hughes movie. But hopefully her bubbe didn't actually feel her up.

Truth is, you should know about Bat Mitzvahs. You should be a maven on Bat Mitzvahs. You had a Bat Mitzvah. But that was a few years and a few hundred Grey Goose sodas ago, so the details are a little fuzzy. Let's review.

In addition to preserving the ancient Jewish tradition of the Hula Hoop contest, Bar and Bat Mitzvahs celebrate a teen's transition into adulthood. Most folks don't realize that Jews automatically become a Bar or Bat Mitzvah on their birthday. They're instant adults. No service, party, or assembly (of Jews) required. So why the big day with the Torah portion, the Electric Slide, and the $18 check from *Zayde* (Grandpa)? The Bar Mitzvah ceremony commemorates the first time a boy chooses to act like an adult and step up to the bimah. After their Bar Mitzvah Day, few men choose to read from the Torah or act like an adult again.

## The Perks
Even so, once they're Bar/Bat Mitzvahed, teens automatically get to do all kinds of supercool stuff they're totally excited about. They can lay tefillin, count in minyans, and read from the Torah. They can own property, testify in a Jewish court, and get married—which they better not do before me. They're held responsible for all their actions, and they're obligated to follow the full catalog of commandments. It's a good deal for the seventh-graders. They can't drive a car, watch an R-rated movie, or buy a six-pack of Goldstar, but they get to uphold 613 laws.

## Fringe Benefits
Many tweens also receive their first *tallit* (or tallis) when they become Bar/Bat Mitzvahs. Worn during morning services, these prayer shawls fulfill the mitzvah of attaching *tzitzit* (fringes) to four-cornered garments as a reminder to observe the commandments. These fringes are what separate the tallis from the Pashmina; of course, depending on the design, they can cost about the same. Some Orthodox men don't wear a tallis until they're married, and some wear a *tallit katan* (small tallit) under their clothes every day, but among modern Heebs, the SuperJew cape comes out on a teen's big day. It's the first time they're called up to the Torah and the first time they're viewed as adults, so it's the first time they get to model the prayer poncho. Traditionally only men wore tallit, but today women do, too. What, like we're going to sit back and watch while the men get to accessorize?

## Ladies First
In fact, all these oh-so-exciting Bar/Bat Mitzvah perks and benefits are distributed according to a ladies-first policy. A girl's granted her Bat Mitzvah status when she turns twelve, but boys don't earn their Bar Mitzvah stripes until they

turn thirteen. Why the age difference? Great Talmudic scholars discovered that Jewish women mature faster than Jewish men. Yeah, I didn't need an ancient rabbi to tell me that: I've got JDate.

## Jewish Grammar 101

I did need a rabbi to tell me that I've been tossing around the phrase "Bar Mitzvah" incorrectly. A *Bar Mitzvah* (son of Commandment) is the awkward boy in the Men's Warehouse suit, not the service he fumbles through. A *Bat Mitzvah* (daughter of Commandment) is the smiley girl in the pink tallis, not the party she invites you to. So, saying "I'm going to a Bat Mitzvah" is wrong, saying "she became a Bat Mitzvah" is right, and uploading my old Bat Mitzvah video to YouTube was just mean. I was going through my awkward phase. My bangs were growing out, my braces were still on, and my Clearasil hadn't kicked in. Why, oh why, was that the most photographed day of my life?

## When, where, wear:

A Bat Mitzvah's an event in two acts; be prepared to play the role of girlfriend in both. On Saturday morning you'll head to synagogue for services. Remember to cover you shoulders, your cleavage, and your mouth when you yawn. The Bat Mitzvah service you'll attend is a standard-issue Shabbat morning service. There's nothing special about it, except for the special guest star. The Bat Mitzvah girl's set list varies from shul to shul, but expect her to rock some combination of an Aliyah, a Haftorah portion, a Torah portion, and a huge sigh of relief.

If the party doesn't immediately follow the service, you're looking at a costume change. Don't throw on any old *schmatte* (rag): wear what you'd wear to a wedding held in that same time slot. A little cocktail dress, a BCBG halter, or the one bridesmaid getup you actually can wear again. Look fun and flirty, but classy. You don't want to be squeezing your poulkes into Forever 21 when you're surrounded by girls who are actually under twenty-one.

The party will be held at the synagogue, a country club, or any banquet hall that can hold a huge group Hora. It usually centers around an over-the-top theme like Brady's Favorite Baseball Teams, Jessica's Favorite Ballerinas, or

Andrew's Favorite Porn Stars. Other party highlights include a candle-lighting ceremony, a band that wasn't good enough to get a wedding gig, and the world's largest sweets table. Expect lots of food, dancing, food, speeches, and food. So bring comfy shoes and a spare pair of Spanx. You should be able to score some drinks, but different from a wedding, a Bar Mitzvah bar is usually pretty limited. So stuff a flask in your tallis bag.

### What to bring:

Be sure to bring a gift. *Alter kockers* (old folks) like to give books, mezuzahs, and Israeli bonds; teenagers like to receive music, clothes, and cash. Try to go in on your date's gift; that way the card is signed from both of you—it's always good to get your relationship in writing.

........................................................................................................................................

## EVENT: SHIVA (SEVEN)
## DESCRIPTION: A SHOW OF SUPPORT
## STARRING: A MOURNING FAMILY
## SIGNIFICANCE: TO HELP THE GRIEVING

It's only funny until someone loses a relative. Then it's hard. But if you're hoping to hear "for better or for worse," be there for him in good times and in bad. If a boyfriend's relative passes away, join him in making a shiva call. Stop by the house, show your support, and since you're already there, you might as well have a little nosh. A few things to know before you go:

- No, his relatives aren't shorter than the average Jew. Mourners sit low to the ground, on small stools or benches, as a sign of grief. That's why it's often called "sitting shiva."

- Shiva is a time for thinking and remembering, not curling and primping. To prevent vanity, mourners cover all their mirrors. So put your lipstick on before you leave the car.

- Knock, knock. Who's there? Doesn't matter. Mourners shouldn't have to play host or greet their guests, so don't ring the bell or knock on the door. Just let yourself in.

- Mourners publicly burn a memorial candle for a week. I'm talking 24/7. So don't blo—too late.

- Mourners perform *kriah* (tearing) on their clothing or a small black ribbon to physically express their anguish and anger; the ripped ribbon is worn throughout shiva. Only immediate family does kriah, so leave your ripped jeans at home. I was kidding. You seriously still own ripped jeans? Wow. Jon Bon Jovi called: even he doesn't want his pants back.

## How can you eat at a time like this?

Jews don't drown our sorrows in alcohol; we smother them with cream cheese. Immediately following the funeral, the community joins the mourners for a big *Seudat Havra'ah* (meal of condolence). There are dessert platters, fruit trays, tuna salad, egg salad, and tons of Jewish comfort food like bagels, lox, and shmear. Some say we serve round foods like bagels to symbolize the circle of life. I say what other shape bagels would we serve? Friends organize, arrange, and pay for this meal, and all of the mourners' meals, all week long.

## When, where, wear:

For the seven days following the funeral, the family sits shiva at the home of the deceased or at a close relative's. Members of the community come by to show their support and comfort the mourners. It's best to make a shiva call in the evening, when the Mourner's Kaddish is recited during a brief Ma'ariv service; but anytime is a good time to show your respect. This is not the time to show your poulkes; so leave your miniskirts and tank tops at home. No need to wear black, just look modest, appropriate, and like you just stepped out of Ann Taylor, J. Crew, or Michelle Obama's closet.

## What to bring:

Before you arrive, give *tzedakah* (righteous giving) to a fitting charity in memory of the person who passed. It's a mitzvah—and it'll make you look good in front of your hopefully future in-laws. Also, bring something sweet to the shiva house. If guests supply dessert, the mourners don't have to stress about feeding everyone who makes a shiva call. Remember to ask if the family keeps kosher before deciding what to bring. Whatever you decide, don't bring flowers; it's very *goyisher kop* (Gentile-thinking). Jews are all about the nosh. A dozen rugelach beat a dozen roses any day.

......................................................................................................................

## EVENT: WEDDINGS
## DESCRIPTION: A GIANT REMINDER THAT YOU'RE STILL SINGLE
## STARRING: EVERYONE BUT YOU
## SIGNIFICANCE: TO CELEBRATE MARRIAGE

You've watched all of your Jewish friends get married and ride off into the sunset—unless they had a Saturday night wedding. In which case, they couldn't get married until after sundown, so they just rode off into the dark. Based on the serious number of hours you've clocked in at weddings, you should be a matrimony maven by now. But you're not, because you usually spend the ceremony deciding which single groomsman to go for. So you still don't know what a little tent, a do-si-do, and breaking barware have to do with getting a guy to marry me. Not me, I mean Jewish girls in general. Obviously I didn't mean me. Based on my dating record, my wedding's going to take place a long, long time from now in a galaxy far, far away. But for everyone else, this is how their upcoming wedding day will go down:

### Pre-Ceremony
#### WEDDING DRESS DIET

On their wedding day the *kallah* (bride) and *chattan* (groom) fast from the moment they wake up until their ceremony is complete. Fast for a day? Oy gevalt! The sensible bride would diet for a minimum of six months if she wants to look svelte in her gown. But if she only fasts for a day, it's because a wedding day is considered a personal Yom Kippur. The bride and groom fast to atone for their sins before starting their brand-new life together. This crash diet not only gives a naughty girl a clean slate but helps her shed those last few pounds, so she's light enough to be lifted in a chair mid-Hora.

## KABBALAT PANIM

A few hours before the ceremony, the kallah and chattan host separate single-sex pre-parties called *Kabbalat Panim*. Close friends and family gather together to celebrate with the bride or groom. There's toasting, drinking, singing, dancing, and noshing. Think of Kabbalat Panim as Jewish bachelor and bachelorette parties. Minus strippers. Plus rugelach.

## SIGN ON THE DOTTED LINE

Next up is the ketubah signing. *Ketubah* comes from the root *Kaf-Tav-Bet*, which means "writing." As in, my dad, a successful Jewish lawyer, taught me to always get things in writing. The *ketubah* is a written marriage contract; a binding legal document that obligates a man to take care of his wife and provide food, clothing, and protection. The sword kind, not the condom kind. Not that Jewish men ever carry either.

The ketubah is also an ancient, one-sided prenup that describes what kind of haul the bride scores in a divorce—traditionally something like ten shekels, four goats, and a pushcart. Today, most couples choose updated ketubah language that describes their mutual love and respect. But if the modern bride's smart, she'll sneak that part about the four goats (his Lexus and the house) in there, too.

Postwedding, couples usually frame their ketubah and hang it prominently in their home. It's a beautiful reminder of their love for each other and a constant reminder that the husband promised to bring home the bacon. Well, not the bacon, because that would be trayf. But he better bring home the brisket. Produce the pastrami. Churn out the cholent.

## BADECKEN (TO COVER OVER)

Our forefather Jacob knew about working hard for the money. He worked his tuchus off for seven years so he could score with Rachel. Such a shayna punim on that one! He won her hand, stood beneath the chuppah, and said yes to a veiled bride. Who turned out to be Rachel's older sister, Leah. D'oh! Jake worked for seven more years so he could finally marry his beloved hot chick, Rachel. To make sure he doesn't get Jacobed, the groom now visits the bride's room and personally veils the right girl. Can't pull the wool—or tulle —over his eyes.

## WALKING THE PLANK

On their wedding day, a Jewish bride and groom are treated like a king and queen. So it's only appropriate that they're escorted down the aisle by an entourage, usually made up of their parents, their friends, and Johnny Drama. The groom goes first; then the bride makes her big entrance.

A Jewish bride will never walk down the aisle to "Here Comes the Bride." Oy gevalt! Your bubbe spits on that song. It was written by Hitler's favorite composer, Richard Wagner. Feh! Expect the bride to enter to a bubbe-approved tune composed by a classy, respectable Jewish composer, like George Gershwin, Irving Berlin, or Gene Simmons.

Once the bride enters the chuppah, she circles the groom seven times. Why? Some say the world was created in seven days, so the bride creates their new life in seven spins. Others say Joshua circled Jericho seven times to bring down the city walls, so the bride circles Joshua, or Bill, or whoever she's marrying, seven times to bring down their emotional walls. I say the bride's modeling her dress for everyone in attendance. That baby cost $2,000, and she's only wearing it once. You bet she's going to do her little turn on the catwalk.

## Ceremony

### KIDDUSHIN

With both the kallah and chattan under the chuppah, the rabbi begins the wedding. A Jewish wedding has two distinct ceremonies. During the *kiddushin* (betrothal), a man calls dibs on a woman by giving her a ring. During the *nis-*

*suin* (nuptials), the man and woman seal the deal with seven blessings. The two ceremonies were once separated by as many as twelve months, so the man could prepare for marriage. Today they're separated by as many as twelve seconds, so the rabbi can read the ketubah. No smart bride's giving her groom twelve months to think about it. How many times have you tried on a dress, told the salesperson you'd think about it, and then actually gone back to buy it? Exactly. We're doing this thing now.

Kiddushin begins with the blessing over the wine. The couple drinks two glasses of wine during their wedding; it's a throwback to the time of two separate ceremonies. Plus the wise rabbis understood that a groom usually needs more than one round in him before he'll find the matzah balls to go through with "I do."

After the wine comes the ring. A Jewish wedding ring must be a plain gold band, no emerald-cut or channel-set diamonds allowed. The uninterrupted circle symbolizes the never-ending love of the couple, and the lack of stones suggests a smooth marriage. The lack of stones also suggests that this will be the least expensive piece of jewelry this man will ever buy his wife. Over the years she'll expect him to compensate for her smooth wedding band with diamond earrings, diamond necklaces, and diamond bracelets. Ironically, this expectation is what often causes the not-so-smooth moments in a marriage.

**NISSUIN**

The second ceremony, nissuin, features the recitation of the *Sheva Brachot* (seven blessings). Yes, there's that number seven again. The first is a blessing over the wine, the second thanks God for creating a glorious world, the third thanks God for creating mankind, the fourth thanks God for creating people in his image, the fifth focuses on Jewish children populating Zion, the sixth centers on the joy of the bride and groom, and the seventh thanks God for creating happiness, friendship, joy, and peace in the world and specifically for the bride and groom. May they live happily ever after.

After the seven blessings, the happy couple kisses, the groom stomps on a glass, and all the guests yell "Mazel Tov!" Why's the groom breaking barware? To remember the destruction of the Temple even in this moment of happiness;

to demonstrate the fragility of marriage even in this moment of true love; and to justify registering for crystal even though the couple will never use it. Seriously, when are they going to need Baccarat? My married friends normally drink Bud Light from the bottle. Okay, fine, they don't, I'm exaggerating. My married friends normally drink Bud Light from the can.

## Postceremony

### GET A ROOM

After the ceremony the Jewlyweds are commanded to spend time alone in *yichud* (seclusion). The bride and groom meet in a private chamber while their guests enjoy the open bar and passed appetizers. In the old days, this is when they consummated the marriage with a quickie. Nowadays, this is when they consummate the marriage with a quickie.

### SO YOU THINK YOU CAN HORA

At the Seudat Mitzvah, we're commanded to celebrate the occasion with a huge meal. We're commanded to entertain the Jewlyweds with song and dance. And we're commanded to get drunk and play spin-the-dreidel with a good-looking groomsman. Okay fine, we're not commanded to fulfill that last bit, but isn't that the whole reason we single girls show up to weddings? I'm not here for the free cake; I'm here to dance the horizontal Hora with the best man.

Speaking of Hora, whose cockamamie idea was it to get all *faputzed* (dressed up) for a wedding and then get jiggy with the Jewish dancing? You start schvitzing, your hair starts frizzing, and it's impossible to do the Hora in four-inch heels. Or is it?

Ladies, you don't have to choose between dancing the Hora and being a hottie. The trick is to keep your weight on the balls of your feet at all times. If you put your heels down, you'll be going down. The savvy Jewess also brings socks or flats to throw on. Your fashion sense takes a dive, but you won't. You'll be Dancing with the (Jewish) Stars.

Got two left stilettos? Not sure of the choreography? Not a problem. The Hora's a simple circle dance. Step to the side with your right and cross your left leg behind, then step to the side again with your right, and cross in front with your left. Got it? No? No worries. Just grab hands with the folks on either side of you; then run when they run, stop when they stop, and kick when they kick. When the music stops, hit the bar for a cold one.

## When, where, wear:

You think it's hard to find a nice Jewish boy to date? You should try finding a date to have your nice Jewish wedding on. Oy! Jewish weddings can't be held during Shabbat, so Friday nights and Saturdays until sundown are off limits. Waiting for three stars to appear in a Saturday night sky can lead to a late start; so many Jews choose to have an early Sunday evening ceremony instead. Sunday of a three-day weekend is considered prime nuptial time because it gives guests an extra day to travel. And an extra day to recover from their hangovers.

Of course, you can't have a wedding on any old Sunday. Jewish wedding blackout dates include all the Jewish holidays, the three weeks leading up to Tisha B'Av (usually in July), and the seven weeks between Passover and Shavuot (usually April–June). Translation: there are a lot of Jewish couples competing for a few choice dates. You better book the Four Seasons for the Sunday night of Labor Day now. I said now. Why are you still sitting here reading? Put down the book and pick up the phone. Who cares if you don't have a groom— go book the room.

If the Four Seasons is booked and the synagogue is too small, couples can hold their wedding in a banquet hall, a country club, or their own backyard. Jewish weddings can be held anywhere, as long as they're held under a *chuppah*. This wedding canopy represents the newlywed's new home. Like Abraham and Sarah's tent, it should be open on four sides. Not that the newlywed's new home should be a tent, or lack four walls, or have fewer than four bedrooms— if the groom knows what's good for him.

No matter where the wedding is held, you should get all dolled up for the event. Not just because it's a fancy occasion, but because you'll want to look your best for those single groomsmen. Come prepared to cover your shoulders during the ceremony out of respect for Jewish custom and out of a wish to stay warm. Outdoor weddings can get chilly, especially if you're sporting a little strapless dress. So make like a challah and cover up.

## What to bring:

Bring a gift. I doubt our ancestors made chicken soup in Le Creuset pots or kneaded challah dough with a KitchenAid mixer. But the registry has become a Jewish wedding tradition, complete with $45 hand-woven placemats, $95 frying pans, and $125 stainless-steel garbage cans. If you cringe at the idea of buying your friend of fifteen years an overpriced place to throw her trash and *chazzerai* (junk), make like Abraham and start a whole new tradition. Ditch the registry and give your friends a Judaica gift. A Jewish-themed gift stands out from the Pottery Barn kitchenware, will actually get used, and your friend won't know exactly how much you spent on her. Shop Judaica stores, synagogue gift shops, and online sites for Shabbat candlesticks, a Kiddush cup, a challah board, a Seder plate, a Havdalah set, a tzedakah box, or a menorah. If you're going for the schmaltzy gift, buy the Jewlyweds a mezuzah or Kiddush cup that's meant to hold the broken glass from their wedding. Nothing says welcome to your Jewish life together like a little Jewish kitsch.

# NOBODY PUTS BAGEL IN THE CORNER

If you're playing plus-guest at a Seudat Mitzvah, you better learn your way around a deli tray. Men take their Jew food seriously, and they want a girl who knows how to nosh. Don't know your farfel from your falafel? Or your kreplach from your kneidlach? Well, help has arrived. This cheat sheet should help you navigate the spread at any Jewish simcha. But remember, it doesn't matter if it's a milk or meat buffet, everything from the deli goes straight to your belly, so go easy on the schmaltzy stuff.

**BAGEL**: This roll with a hole is boiled, then baked.

**BIALY**: This roll with no hole plays backup to the bagel.

**BLINTZ**: A blintz is a Jewish crepe . . . and a beret is a French kippah.

**BORSCHT**: This cold beet soup is the Jewish gazpacho.

**BOUREKAS**: The Hebrew Hot Pocket, it's usually filled with spinach, potato, or cheese.

**BRISKET**: This braised beef is a favorite at holiday meals with the mishpacha.

**CHICKEN SOUP**: Also known as the Jewish penicillin, the kosher cold remedy, and in prescription form, Bubbemycin.

**CHOLENT**: This stew simmers overnight so a hostess can serve a hot Shabbat lunch without working on the Sabbath. Of course, getting through a bowl of cholent usually requires work on the guest's part.

**CHOPPED LIVER**: It's the frum foie gras.

**CORNED BEEF**: The crown jewel of the Jewish deli, it's brisket that's been brined, then steamed. Ladies, if you bring your guy a hot corned beef on rye, you may win his heart for life.

**CREAM CHEESE (SHMEAR)**: It's all about accessorizing. You wouldn't buy a dress without matching shoes, so, nu, why would you eat a bagel without shmear?

**CREAMED HERRING**: This onion, fish, and sour cream dish is a staple at simchas.

**FALAFEL**: These Chickpea McNuggets come with your choice of dipping sauces: hummus, tahini, and babaganoush.

**GEFILTE FISH**: Who doesn't love a little fish loaf? This Jew food specialty is cooked with ground carrots, onions, and whitefish, pike, or carp. The old-school balabusta makes it from scratch; the trendy yenta makes it from the jar.

**HORSERADISH SAUCE**: Horseradish is to gefilte fish what wasabi is to sushi.

**HUMMUS**: This chickpea spread is the Israeli mayo.

**ISRAELI SALAD**: Sliced 'n' diced tomatoes, cucumbers, lemon juice, and olive oil. This salad is a health oasis in a sea of carbs and schmaltz.

**KASHA VARNISHKES**: Made from buckwheat, pasta, onions, and schmaltz ... you know it's a formal occasion when even your buckwheat is wearing a bowtie.

**KISHKE AND GRAVY**: The original "don't ask, don't tell." But if you must know, a cow intestine stuffed with matzah meal, schmaltz, and seasonings. Today, synthetic casings replace the real stuff, so you can eat every bite of this delish side dish.

**KNEIDLACH (MATZAH BALLS)**: Don't squeeze his matzah balls. Enough said.

**KNISH**: Like a kosher calzone, this tasty turnover is stuffed with potato, meat, or cheese.

**KREPLACH**: The Jewish wonton.

**KUGEL**: Not to be confused with the feminine exercises.... This casserole can be made with noodles or potatoes, eaten hot or cold, and spiced savory or sweet. Oy vey, so many choices, who can decide? Jewish tradition says take one of each.

**LATKES**: The Hebrew hash brown.

**LOX**: Sliced smoked salmon. You rarely see lox without his best buddy bagel; those two are joined at the shmear.

**MATZAH FARFEL**: Jews put the "oy" in oyster cracker with these tiny pieces of matzah that float in chicken soup.

**PASTRAMI**: Sliced brisket that's been brined, dried, seasoned, and smoked. Grab a little mustard, a little rye, and a pickle on the side, and you're good to go.

**RUGELACH**: Made with chocolate, cinnamon, or preserves, these little rolled cookies pack a big taste. And a big calorie count, so watch it....

**SHAWARMA**: Seasoned beef, chicken, or lamb that sits 'n' spins on a spit.

**SMOKED FISH**: Thank you for smoking ... white-fish that is.

**TAM TAMS**: This kosher cracker makes the perfect chopped liver or herring picker-upper. So please, don't eat with your fingers in front of his mishpacha.

# CHAPTER 3

# SHUL HOUSE ROCK
## (SYNAGOGUE)

Dan and I met at a speaker series seven years ago; it was rabbi at first sight. A Scotch-drinking, basketball-playing, Torah-quoting mensch, he was a rabbi I could relate to. He invited me to Shabbat dinner, included me in his study group, and introduced me to his family—which is always a big step in a relationship. One Hamotzi lead to another, and next thing I knew, I had myself a spiritual leader. No, more than that, I had myself a friend. Wow, I'm the one who wrote that sentence and it sounds cheesy even to me, which I guess is fine as long as I don't follow it with meat. Actually, I'll follow it with Nate.

Nate and I met at a party three weeks ago. A Reform rabbi with a goatee, he runs a rocking singles' Shabbat service at a nearby shul. I accepted his invitation to check it out sometime. And that's when I felt it, that funny feeling in my stomach, the same funny feeling I get when I meet a guy at a bar and accidentally totally on purpose forget to tell him I'm already seeing someone. Why didn't I tell Nate I already have a rabbi? Why didn't I admit that I was good in the Shabbat department? Why didn't I mention I'm a life-long Conservative?

Well, I've gotten myself into a fine kettle of smoked fish. Let's say I go to Nate's Friday night service and to Dan's for Shabbos lunch. What do I do if Dan asks where I was last night? Do I tell him the truth? That I was with another rabbi, but it didn't mean anything? What if Dan asks how the service was? Do I tell him it was different? That his is better?

Oy to the Vey. I'm used to multidating, I'm used to seeing other people, I always have a lot of matzah balls in the air. But that's dating, not praying. When it comes to Judaism, is it appropriate to have an open relationship? Can I see other synagogues? Can I be involved with other rabbis?

Up to this point, I've always been a spiritual monogamist, a one-rabbi kind of girl. My parents helped start our shul, and I was in preschool when they picked our rabbi. He was at my brother's bris, he was on the bimah at my Bat Mitzvah, and he led every Shabbat service I attended. Since moving to L.A., Dan's been the man. He offers me guidance, encourages my questions, and I always assumed he'd officiate my wedding. Not that I ever think about my wedding, or where I'd register (Crate and Barrel), or where I'd have it (the beach).

And now I'm in double trouble. Since my tsouris is steeped in Judaism, I should probably turn to the Torah for help. What do the ancient texts say about double-dipping in the rabbi department? Not much. The Ten Commandments are very clear that we should only have one God. But they don't say anything about only one rabbi or only one shul. And it seems like the rest of Judaism is chock-full of twos. We're told to have two sets of dishes, two Shabbat challahs, and two Shabbat candles. So, nu, what would be so wrong with two rabbis?

*Rabbi* comes from the word *rav*, meaning "teacher." One can never have too many teachers. In high school I didn't take English from my science teacher, and in college I had a plethora of professors. So having more than one rabbi or attending more than one shul should actually round out my Jewish education.

So it's settled; I won't put all my rabbis in one basket. I'm going to keep my options open, switch up shuls, and mix up minyans. I'm going to Shabbos-hop without guilt and service-surf at my whim. Dan will always be my go-to guy, but I'm free to see other rabbis on the side. Because as a great rabbi once wrote, variety is the schmaltz of life.

••••••••••••••••••••••••••••••••••••••••••••••••••••••••••

# THERE'S NO PLACE LIKE SHUL

I may be into seeing several synagogues, but I can't say the same for everyone else. Synagogue is the last place some young Jews want to spend their free time. They're still suffering from bad childhood flashbacks. You wake up late for shul and you don't want to go, you ask your *ima* (mom) please, but she still says no. Sound familiar? You probably spent many a dreaded Sunday morning and one or two boring afternoons a week zoning out in Hebrew School. You learned how to read a few prayers and sing a few songs, but mostly you looked forward to the ten-minute break when you could eat your kosher snack. Well, synagogue isn't just the place where your parents dragged you for Hebrew School; it's also the religious and social anchor of a Jewish community. It's the hub of a Jewish hood. It's the Peach Pit of the pious. It functions as *Beit Tefilah* (House of Prayer), a *Beit Midrash* (House of Study), and a *Beit K'nesset* (House of Gathering). And any place where eligible Jewish guys and other fun Jewish gals are gathering is a place where you should be. So hi-ho, hi-ho, it's off to shul you go. . . .

••••••••••••••••••••••••••••••••••••••••••••••••••••••••••

# BEIT TEFILAH (HOUSE OF PRAYER)

A synagogue's first function is religious. It's a place where Jews go to get their God on. It's a place where Jews go to pray. Well, maybe not where you go to pray. Outside of Yom Kippur and your third cousin Benji's Bar Mitzvah, you swore you'd never sit through another service again. All I'm saying is give prayer a chance. Services can be inspiring, centering, and even a good time. Check out a summer service held under the stars. Try a bentsch-and-brunch that's followed by bagels. Or hit up a Carlebach minyan that's equal parts Haight-Ashbury and Mogen David Blackberry. Sure, some sermons will put you to sleep faster than an Ambien, and some have more strollers than *siddurs* (prayer books), but all services are not created equal.

## FRIDAY NIGHT SERVICES

Welcome in Shabbat with a little Shul House Rock. Many synagogues offer a modern Friday night service specifically for Jews in their twenties and thirties. With names like Friday Night Live, Finally Friday, and Shabbat Unplugged, these vibrant services often feature rock bands or musicians, are followed by a complimentary cocktail hour, and are led by energetic, inspiring rabbis. All the standard Shabbat fare is there, but it's presented in a way that's accessible, irreverent, and entertaining to Jews who spend their Friday nights at shul and their Saturday nights at bars. In some cities these happening services draw a few hundred or even a few thousand young Jews. That's a lot of circumcised men to choose from. Forget Tot Shabbat, this is hot Shabbat.

## SATURDAY MORNING SERVICES

Wake up and smell the Musaf. Starting as early as 9 AM, Shabbat morning services are made up of two parts, *Shacharit* (morning) and *Musaf* (additional). They feature the weekly Torah portion, a Bar or Bat Mitzvah ceremony, and top ten prayers like the Shema, the Amidah, and Ein Keloheinu. To engage all their members, many congregations offer a full menu of morning choices. You can start your day with a straightforward service in the main sanctuary, a lay-led service in the small sanctuary, or an alternative service in the courtyard. Looking to amp up Shabbat? Seek out your synagogue's Kiddush Club, where members sneak off to a side room and *daven* (pray) while downing shots of Slivovitz. Kiddush Clubs are how the Chosen People choose to get their drink on before noon. L'chaim!

## DAILY MORNING MINYAN

Starting daily around 7 AM, these rise-and-shine services tend to be brief, to-the-point, and have a "just the facts, ma'am" feel. Observant Jews stop by to fulfill their daily davening quota while grieving Jews attend to recite the Mourner's Kaddish. There will always be a *minyan* (quorum of ten Jewish adults) present, but there won't always be a rabbi. These services are commonly congregant-led. Held before the workday begins, the morning minyan is often followed by a brief breakfast. Getting ten people to temple that early can be a challenge, and we're not above bribing with bagels.

## JEW IT YOURSELF

At times services at a super-sized shul can come across as intimidating and impersonal. It's easy to feel like a small gefilte fish in a big sea. That's where Indie Minyans and *Chavurah* (fellowship) groups come in. Twenty to thirty young congregants get together in their homes for Shabbat dinners, holiday celebrations, and living room learning. These *haimesh* (homey), intimate gatherings lead to close friendships and help folks practice Judaism indie-style. Self-led, each group decides what to recite, where to meet, and what to eat. It's perfect for Jews who think outside the tzedakah box.

# BEIT K'NESSET (HOUSE OF GATHERING)

The synagogue isn't just a place to pray; it's also a place to play. Part rec center, part student union, part Jewish day camp, it's a place where members can meet up, hang out, and have fun. Between softball games, barbecues, and book clubs, you can fill your social calendar, jumpstart your love life, and meet fellow Jews while doing things you enjoy. Here are a few ways to get involved:

# JUPPIES (JEWISH URBAN PROFESSIONALS)

With alt rockers replacing alter kockers as the next generation Jew, synagogues are courting Hebrew hipsters. They hope to help members like you explore Jewish life through temple-based activities. Aimed at members ages 21 to 40, these dynamic young adult groups coordinate camping trips, concert nights, baseball games, and ski weekends. It's like USY for young professionals, which means you might get to kiss Brent Fine in the back of the bus on the way to a comedy club. Some things never change.

# THE DIVINE SECRETS OF THE BETH AM SISTERHOOD

If you're part of a congregation, the Sisterhood is a fast path to new friends. This women's group oversees shul-wide projects like the Purim carnival, the Chanukah bazaar, and the weekly *Oneg Shabbat* (post-Shabbat reception). They host ladies-only luncheons, fashion shows, and community service days. They coordinate the congregation cookbook and run the all-important synagogue gift shop. And like *The Sisterhood of the Traveling Kippah*, they organize women-only weekend retreats and weeklong missions to Israel.

# THE CHUTZPAH OF HOPE

Were you elected student council president? AE Phi secretary? SDT social chair? Well, don't let that good leadership experience go to waste: run for an office on the temple board. Just like student government, the synagogue board is involved in fundraising, strategic planning, and overall direction of the congregation. With committees covering ways and means, membership, outreach, education, and social action, the board works closely with the rabbi, cantor, and temple staff to keep the synagogue running smoothly and congregants feeling happy. It's all very *Mr. Stein goes to Washington*.

## HEBREW SCHOOL MUSICAL

Do you miss the days of glee club and jazz hands? Then join the congregation chorus. Giving command performances at Shabbat services, the annual Chanukah concert, and various festivals throughout the year, the choir's a way to meet other talented Jews and launch your comeback tour. If you're lucky, you may even get to star in the synagogue production of *Fiddler on the Roof* or *Joseph and the Amazing Technicolor Dreamcoat*. Talk about a dream come true. . . .

## MIND, BODY, AND SHUL

Were you more of a jock than a band geek? Then sign up for synagogue sports. Stop laughing—congregations offer running clubs, weekly hikes, and even yoga classes. So you can do the downward dog at the place where you daven. Many shuls also sponsor synagogue softball leagues and member basketball teams—proving Jew boys can jump. Congregations compete against their cross-town rivals for synagogue bragging rights. B'nai Tikvah vs. Beth Shalom, Temple Emanuel vs. Temple Sinai, Beth Judea vs. Young Israel. Temple teams are a great way for you to get in shape and meet great guys from multiple congregations. So throw on your running shoes and Just Jew It.

• • • • • • • • • • • • • • • • • • • • • • • • • • • • • • • • • • • • • • • • • • • • • • • • • •

# BEIT MIDRASH (HOUSE OF STUDY)

Synagogues aren't just a house of flirting; they're also a house of learning. Congregations pride themselves on their dedication to education. So make like Thorten Melon and go back to shul. You may not conquer the Triple Lindy, but you can master the double mitzvah. You can take adult courses, increase your Jewish IQ, and have after-hours study sessions with smart, single Jewish men. Sure, you need extra help with your Hebrew homework. . . .

# TEXTING

Don't know your Torah from your Talmud? Your Mishnah from your Midrash? Your tuchus from your Tanakh? In the beginning Jews created lots of books; which means we have a lot to learn. Often taught by a rabbi, these classes go to the heart of Judaism and cover the weekly Torah portion, the great rabbis' commentaries, and the ancient texts upon which our religion is based. Understanding these sacred books will make services more meaningful for you. Or at least a little less boring.

# RE-JEWVENATE

Feeling burnt out on services? Take a break, catch up on culture, and connect to Judaism in a new way. Synagogues host film clubs, book clubs, and lecture series. They run courses in Jewish music, history, and art and offer classes in conversational Hebrew and Yiddish. The cost of these classes is often included in your membership dues. So, nu, why not enroll? You can strengthen your Jewish identity, get active in the temple community, and become a modern maven on all things Jewish. And who knows, you just might meet a mensch while doing so.

# JUDAISM 101

Ever wonder why we light Shabbat candles or how to keep a kosher kitchen? Are you curious why we build a sukkah and celebrate Simchat Torah? Do you want the behind-the-scenes story on all those "they tried to kill us, we survived, let's eat" holidays? Introduction to Judaism classes are a back-to-basics look at Jewish life. Covering Jewish fundamentals like holidays, life-cycle events, and essential prayers and practices, these courses are popular with people considering conversion and adults looking to understand the why behind our rituals. Think of these classes as *Life, Love, Lox* live.

# SHUL-SHOPPING

Now that you're a maven on synagogues, it's time to find a place to hang your kippah. And believe me, it's not one-shul-fits-all. Growing up, you belonged to the temple your parents picked out, but now it's time to find a congregation to call your own. Not sure where to start looking? Not sure you want to start looking? Shopping for a temple is like shopping for a dress—you have to try on a few before finding one that fits. Does this congregation feel good? Is it too small? Does it make my tuchus look big?

When searching for your shulmate, try to attend services and social events at several different places. As you temple-hop, be sure to get the full scoop on each synagogue. . . and maybe hit up their in-house yenta for some good shul gossip.

**THE RABBI**: Do you connect with the rabbi? Do you like the tone he or she sets for the congregation? Can you imagine this rabbi giving you advice? Can you imagine this rabbi officiating your wedding? If so, stop daydreaming about marriage and start focusing on the service.

**THE SERVICE**: Are you enjoying the service? Can you even understand it? Is there too much Hebrew? Too much English? Do congregants sit back and listen or engage and sing along? Do they have a cantor? Do they have a solid Oneg Shabbat spread? You can tell a lot about a synagogue from their mini gefilite fish balls and pareve shul brownies.

**THE SEXES**: Do men and women sit separately? Do they say the names of the *Imahot* (Sarah, Rebecca, Rachel, and Leah) alongside the *Avot* (Abe, Ike, and Jake)? Are women called up to read from the Torah? Do women cover their legs, their heads, or nothing at all?

**THE CONGREGANTS**: Do some people-watching. Do you see other young members or just alter kockers? Are there more families with babies or bachelors with bodies? Does the synagogue have an active young adult group? A strong singles' scene? A strong selection of men? On a scale of one to chai, how good-looking are the guys?

**THE LOGISTICS**: How large is the congregation? Do they own their own building or hold grassroots services in a school gymnasium? Do they meet at a convenient location? Jewish geography is important. So is parking.

**THE COST**: Do a price-check. How much are young membership dues? Do they include High Holiday tickets? What else do dues cover? Can you afford to join this shul and still buy that dress on the mannequin?

## WHAT'S YOUR TYPE?

Single Jewish Female seeking synagogue. Candidates should be down-to-earth, friendly, and egalitarian. Applicants should be bilingual (English and Hebrew) and somewhat conservative. Must respect tradition, but know how to have fun. Youthful personality required, low membership dues preferred. Please, no weirdos.

Not sure what your temple type is? While every shul is unique, most congregations fit into one of five categories: Orthodox, Conservative, Reform, Reconstructionist, and Sephardic/Mizrahi. Ranging from traditional to progressive, each community has its own approach to spirituality and its own take on the Commandments. Congregations within each group vary from one another, but in general, here's how they break down:

### Orthodox

Tradition, baby! Orthodox Jews believe God wrote the whole Torah and passed it all along to Moses on Mount Sinai. God gave him the written Torah, the Oral Torah, the commentaries, the whole kibbitz and caboodle—word for word, story for story, scroll for scroll. And the Big Guy's book has been on the bestseller list ever since. Knowing the Torah was written by an Almighty author, Orthodox Jews take all 613 of its *mitzvot* (commandments) literally. They uphold *halacha* (Jewish law) in the strictest sense and abide by the letter of the law as written. Orthodox Jews keep kosher in and out of their homes, cover their *keppes* (heads) all day long, and don't work, drive, or spark electricity on Shabbat. Know before you go: dress is conservative, and you won't be seated next to any fine-looking frums. In the name of modesty, women aren't called up to the Torah, and a *mechitza* (partition) separates the sexes. But it's fun to spend services guessing which hot bachelor is behind curtain number one.

## Reform

Jewish Star (Trek): The Next Generation. Enlightenment-era rabbis wanted to reconcile Jewish life with their rapidly changing world. They wanted to uphold Jewish ideals while taking part in society at-large. Simply put, they wanted to get with the times, man.

For these rabbis, the revelation didn't end with Moses on Mount Sinai and Jewish law wasn't set in stone. The Torah was a product of the time it was written in; so halacha could be changed to reflect the times they lived in. The rabbis lifted Shabbat restrictions, introduced mixed-sex seating, and switched to non-Hebrew language services. Initially the movement also rejected mitzvot like keeping kosher, donning tallit, and wearing kippot. Today, the Reform movement no longer frowns upon these commandments. Instead it encourages individuals to study Jewish law and then pick and choose which rituals they personally want to practice. Keeping kosher, wearing a tallit, covering your head—it's up to you. If the kippah fits, wear it. If not, that's okay. Whatever you think helps you be Jewish. Reform services are conducted mostly in English and are attended by nice Jewish guys who may—or may not—grab a slice of pepperoni pizza after praying.

## Conservative

*Like The Bridge on the River Chai*, Conservative Judaism popped up in the nineteenth century to connect the two extremes. Many Jews felt the Orthodox's strict interpretation of the law was unrealistic in modern times, but the Reform's dismissal of some commandments went too far. Suffering from religious whiplash, the Conservative movement established itself on middle ground and restored halacha across the board. Welcome home, Hebrew. It's good to see you again, kosher. Say hello to my little friend, tallit. The Conservative movement says Jews are bound by the Torah and all 613 of its mitzvot, but the commandments can be shaped slightly to reflect the times. Individual Jews can't choose which laws to follow, but the rabbis can interpret laws in innovative ways so they make sense in the modern world. You can drive to services on Shabbat, but you still shouldn't work on the day of rest. Men have to wear kippot in shul, but they don't have to cover their keppes all day, every day. In general, the Conservative movement looks to preserve Jewish law while taking it with a grain of kosher salt.

## Reconstructionist

There's a new Jew in town. Formally founded in the 1960s, the Reconstructionist movement views Judaism as an ever-evolving culture, rather than a religion. They think of God as a process, not a personality. The smallest of the movements, members look to continually reconstruct Jewish thought while upholding Jewish tradition. The Torah and commandments weren't created by God, but they should be followed out of respect for Jewish culture. Reconstructionists don't pray to God but instead hope that their prayers awaken something inside themselves. As all modern movements should, Reconstructionist Jews come with their own T-shirt–ready tagline: "The Past has a Vote, not a Veto."

## Sephardic and Mizrahi

Like a feast from the east, these congregations are filled with the spirit, flavor, and spice of Jews who descend from Spain, Portugal, Israel, North Africa, and the Middle East. Sephardim have the same beliefs as Ashkenazim and their temples tend to be traditional, but they bring their own flare to Jewish culture and practices. Sephardim eat *kitniyot* (beans, corn, rice, soy, peanuts, and legumes) during Passover, hold the Torah erect while reading it, and when it comes to prayers, they're singing a different tune. In addition to Hebrew, it's also common to hear Ladino, Spanish, Turkish, Greek, Arabic, Farsi, and French spoken in synagogue. And different than their Ashkenazic counterparts, Sephardic synagogues aren't divided into movements. The U.S. Sephardic community is far from new; in fact, the first North American congregation, Shearith Israel, was Sephardic. In 1492 Columbus sailed the ocean blue. And in 1654 Shearith Israel opened its door. Located in Manhattan, the synagogue is still going strong today.

## TO JOIN OR NOT TO JOIN

You don't need to belong to a synagogue to attend services. You can chant the Amidah, sing Adon Olam, and enjoy the Oneg Shabbat spread without dropping a dime. But temple membership has its privileges. Joining a synagogue makes you part of a team; you become an official member of the community. You can take classes, join social groups, and wear a Members-Only Tallis. You'll be more inspired to get involved, you'll feel a part of something larger, and you'll have the support of fellow congregants who have your back. When you're a Jew, you're a Jew all the way, from your first Slivovitz, to your last dying day....

But aren't membership dues expensive? Joining a synagogue doesn't have to cost you an arm and a poulke. Yes, annual fees can be steep (from $150 to $1,000 for individuals), but they're also somewhat flexible. Most shuls offer dues on a sliding scale and have low young adult rates for folks under 35. So you don't have to be a chai roller to be part of a congregation.

## WHY PAY TO PRAY?

That being said, you should still fork over as much as you can afford to; synagogues rely on your dues to survive. The funds go toward the shul's mortgage, insurance, utilities, and upkeep. They pay for the books in the library, the couches in the lobby, and the rabbi on the bimah. They cover the cost of the siddurs, kippot, tallit, and even the bobby pins that hold down your little lace doily. You have a gym membership, a AAA membership, and a Costco card, so why not splurge for a shul membership? If you can buy your Charmin in bulk, you can buy your services in bulk. Besides, your temple membership is tax-deductible. Even the U.S. government wants you to enlist.

# A SHUL BY ANY OTHER NAME . . .

Enlist in what—a synagogue? A shul? What about a Beit K'nesset, a temple, or The Temple? What's the difference? The difference is in the person speaking. They all refer to a Jewish house of worship. *Beit K'nesset* is Hebrew, *shul* is Yiddish, *synagogue* is Greek, and *temple* is a little controversial. The Temple with a capital T refers specifically to the ancient synagogue in Jerusalem that was destroyed, rebuilt, and destroyed again. While observant Jews only use the word Temple to describe the Big One, the Reform movement started using it to describe any Jewish house of worship. Like Kleenex and Xerox, the proper name became the common name, and today the word *temple* has street cred amongst non–Orthodox Jews.

# JEWISH PICKUP LINES

We've all been there. You spot a handsome man across the bar, but you can't come up with a witty line, so you just let him walk away. Well, ladies, that kind of flirt-and-run accident doesn't happen in shul. If you spot a handsome man across the bimah, you're in luck. "Don't talk to strangers" doesn't apply in temple. It's perfectly acceptable—in fact, *encouraged*—to throw out a Jewish greeting to someone you've never seen before. There's no awkward introduction; you don't have to wedge your way next to him while ordering a drink. You can head straight toward him at the Oneg, open with the appropriate Jewish greeting, and then flirt away. Haven't tossed out a shul greeting since Hebrew School? Here are a few Jew lines that could come in handy:

## GENERAL:

**"SHALOM" ("HELLO," "GOODBYE," "PEACE"):** This little pickup line goes a long way. One word and you're in.

**"L'CHAIM" ("TO LIFE"):** He's already double-fisting the Mogen David, so your job is that much easier. Here's to life, love, and the pursuit of marriageness!

**"LAILA TOV" ("GOOD NIGHT"):** Perfect for when you're saying goodbye to him after Friday night services or falling asleep next to him after doing the double mitzvah.

**"BOKER TOV" ("GOOD MORNING"):** Try this when you meet a man at Saturday morning services or when you wake up in bed next to him the following day. "Boker Tov, baby, do you want me to make some coffee?"

**"MAZEL TOV" ("GOOD LUCK"):** Say this to a man who just had good luck. It's usually used to congratulate him on his recent wedding, his new baby, or his son's Bar Mitzvah, but it can also be used with regards to a new job, a new home, or any exciting event. For example, "Mazel Tov on meeting your future wife . . . me!"

**"MA NISHMA" ("WHAT'S NEW?"):** The rabbi's way of saying "Whazzup?"

## SHABBAT:

**"SHABBAT SHALOM" ("SABBATH PEACE," "SABBATH GOOD-BYE," OR "SABBATH HELLO"):** It's simple, to the point, and works way better than "Hey there, handsome, want to bimah my little baby?"

**"GUT SHABBOS" ("GOOD SABBATH"):** Shabbat Shalom with a Yiddish twist. Stick with me, honey, and I'll show you a good Shabbos. . . .

**"YASHER KOACH" ("INCREASED STRENGTH," "GOOD JOB"):** Toss this out after he completes a Mitzvah like opening the Ark or reading the Torah. Not that he needs to increase his strength, or go to the gym, or start working out, because his tuchus already looks tight in the suit he wore to services.

**"SHAVUA TOV" ("GOOD WEEK"):** This is the perfect line to use if you see him at a Havdalah ceremony. Hey, good-looking, have a good week.

**"IS THIS SEAT TAKEN?":** If you spot him on your way into services, snag the seat next to him. Then look him in the eye, do a little hair flip, and in your sexiest whisper ask, "What page are we on?"

## ALL HOLIDAYS:

**"CHAG SAMEACH" ("HAPPY HOLIDAY"):** This is all you need to get your high heel in the door with a synagogue stud.

**"GUT YONTIF" ("GOOD HOLIDAY"):** This catch-all Yiddish phrase is a line for all seasons. Now that he's met you, it will be a good holiday ...

## ROSH HASHANAH:

**"L'SHANAH TOVAH" ("HAPPY NEW YEAR"):** Wish your handsome new man a Happy New Year.

**"G'MAR CHATIMAH TOVAH" ("MAY YOU BE SEALED IN THE BOOK OF LIFE"):** Drop this line while kibbitzing over honey cake, and you may have yourself a new honey.

## YOM KIPPUR:

**"TZOM KAL" ("EASY FAST"):** Not to be confused with, "I'm easy," which also works well.

**"L'SHANAH TOVAH TIKATEVU V'TECHATEMU" ("MAY YOU BE INSCRIBED AND SEALED FOR A GOOD YEAR"):** If you can get this tongue-twister out, you've already shown him you're good with your mouth.

## CHANUKAH:

**"HAPPY CHANUKAH"**: Let him know he can spin you like a dreidel anytime.

## PASSOVER:

**"CHAG KASHER V'SAMEACH" ("WISHING YOU A KOSHER AND HAPPY PASSOVER")**: Say this to a guy you don't want to pass over.

**"HAPPY PASSOVER"**: Like matzah, this opening line is a little bland—but not if you follow it with "I'll take you to the Promised Land."

# CHAPTER 4

# TOO COOL FOR SHUL
## (COMMUNITY INVOLVEMENT)

That's it! I'm done. I'm throwing in the tallis. I can hit up bars and clubs until the kosher cows come home, I'm never going to meet a good guy. A schmuck? Sure. A mensch? No. Have you been to the bars lately? It's like close encounters of the worst kind out there. If God created those men in his image, well, that's not saying much for God.

"Why don't you try something different? Take a class? Or volunteer?" asks my mom when I call her to kvetch long-distance. "You could make some friends, do some good, and who knows, maybe meet a good guy."

She's right; I should give up the bar scene and give something back. And I know exactly how to do it. I sit on a leadership council at The Jewish Federation. We do charity work, plan social events, and hold really long board meetings where people ramble on. This weekend we're running an outdoor sports day for at-risk youths. So I can work on my mitzvot and my tan—perfect! Armed with my new attitude, a Chicago Bears tee, and some low-slung jeans, I head out to make a difference. And meet a different kind of man.

I get to the volunteer event and throw myself into my coach-for-a-day duties. I teach my team of youths that no matter what happens, they should have fun, work together, and most important, never lose. Wow, I'm good at helping others. I'm like a regular Yenta Teresa over here.

Somewhere between the water-balloon toss and the potato-sack race, this fine board member I've never met before walks up to me. "Hi, I'm Todd. You're from Chicago, right? I'm having a bunch of people over later to watch the Bulls in the playoffs. You should come."

Looks like Mother knows best. It's not that there are no good guys out there; I'm just looking for "like" in all the wrong places. Men at bars only want to pick up one thing—and it's not the tab. But men at volunteer events are clearly different. Todd didn't make a move; he didn't use a cheesy line; this isn't even a date. He's hosting a big group of volunteers at his place, and he's kind enough to include me—what a mensch.

I'm the first to arrive at Todd's. He hands me a beer, I plop down on his couch, and we start chitchatting. And chitchatting. Twenty minutes later we're still alone chitchatting.

"Let's start watching the game," he suggests, "and let everyone else catch up when they get here."

First Quarter: We cheer on the Bulls, trade travel stories, and discover we're both lifelong Cubs fans—which speaks volumes about his ability to stick with a relationship even through the hard times.

Second Quarter: The Bulls are looking good and so is Todd. He laughs at all my jokes, melts me with his smile, and amazes me with his optimism. He's clearly the kind of man who wakes up every morning with a positive outlook. Not that I plan to be there when he wakes up or have even pictured him in bed. Well, now I am.

Third Quarter: I just realized something. I'm not the first person to arrive; I'm the only person to arrive. Nobody else is coming over. Nobody else was ever coming over. I'm such a schnook. Todd didn't invite me to watch basketball because he's a total mensch; he invited me because he thinks I'm an easy layup.

I can't believe I fell for his line. I'm not some Chaim Yankel fresh off the bus. I'm smarter than the average dater. I know not to go home with some hot guy I just met. Yet here I am all alone in a near-stranger's apartment, and my only weapon is the empty beer bottle in my hand. Great, I'm defenseless and a little buzzed.

And I'm disappointed. I thought I met a mensch who's saving the world one relay race at a time. But no, Todd is just seducing the world one shayna punim at a time. Granted, of all the girls at the volunteer event, he did seduce me. That's flattering.

"So, where's everyone else?" I ask tentatively.

"I don't know. They were supposed to be here, Scott, Isaac, all of them. I swear."

Well, I've gotten myself into quite the kosher pickle. I want to believe his story, I do. It's not like Todd joined J-Fed a year ago so he could wake up super-early on a Sunday and lure me to his lair. He got involved because tikkun olam and tzedakah are important to him. And while *tzedakah* is often translated as "charity," it comes from the root *Tzadei-Dalet-Qof*, meaning "fair" or "just." And it would be unjust of me to judge Todd on what could be a total misunderstanding. It would be unfair of me to assume he was making a schmaltzy move. Maybe I'm being too hard on him. Maybe I'm making a mistake. Maybe I'm watching a great guy walk away. I'm definitely watching a great tuchus walk away. Wow. Sorry, I got distracted. Where was I?

I decide to stay for the rest of the game: good play call on my part. The Bulls win the game, and Todd wins my heart. On my way out the door, I volunteer to see him again. Months later we're still going strong. There's something to this idea of contributing to the Jewish community and making the world a better place. Think globally, date locally.

......................................................

# CHECK YOUR LOCAL LISTINGS

From volunteer events to adventure trips, fundraisers to foodies' nights, there are countless ways to join up with the Jewish community. It doesn't matter if you're a fairly observant Jew or a Chanukah-only girl, community organizations are equal-opportunity enjoyers. Think you're too cool for shul? Great! You don't need to be connected to a congregation to be a part of the community. These groups exist outside the synagogue system, so you can create a dynamic and meaningful Jewish life that actually means something to you. You can connect to Jewish culture in a real way and make this religion your own. So what are you waiting for? Get off your tuchus, and go get your Jew on.

# COMMUNITY SERVICE ORGANIZATIONS

Jewish service organizations are the perfect way to meet a nice Jewish boy while doing something nice. You can kill two birds with one stone, although I don't think killing birds or throwing stones makes for great community service. Usually Jews stick to more civil means like *tzedakah* (righteous giving), *gemilut chasadim* (acts of lovingkindness), and *tikkun olam* (healing the world). So put down the rock and come lend a hand.

## TZEDAKAH

Want to help the community? You can start by shaking your moneymaker. *Tzedakah* refers to giving that is not only charitable, but just, fair, and right. Jews believe giving money to the poor is the right thing to do. We also believe giving money to Bloomingdale's is the right thing to do—especially if you find that perfect little black dress that you can wear day into night and pair with flip-flops or heels. But giving to the poor is good, too. In fact, it's more than good; it's necessary. Jews are commanded to do the righteous thing. We're obligated to help people in need; even the poor are commanded to give money to those who are even less fortunate than themselves.

So how much are you in for? Traditionally, Jews donate ten percent of their salary. The great rabbinic scholars are still debating if that's pre- or post-taxes. If you can't afford to give ten percent, give five, or two, or at least give something. Don't be a chazzer. Even on a cubicle-earned salary, you can give a little bit of cash to someone who's a lot more in need. Open up your Kate Spade wallet, and donate the cost of your latte addiction for a month, the damage you do at the bars in a night, or what you spend on your mani-pedi every week. It's time to put your money where your mouth is. Unless your mouth is kissing some random guy right now, in which case finish that, and then go give tzedakah.

## GEMILUT CHASADIM

Tzedakah's necessary, but it's not enough. Actions speak louder than gelt, so get ready for *gemilut chasadim* (acts of lovingkindness). These good deeds go beyond just giving money and engage a person to give of themselves. Traditionally, there are six gemilut chasadim: clothing the poor, visiting the sick, attending a funeral, supporting mourners, providing food and lodging, and sponsoring a poor bride's wedding. You heard correctly, right up there with providing food, clothing, and shelter is paying for a wedding. Makes sense, right? Who needs a roof over her head when she can have a chuppah over it instead? So some poor guy needs clothing—this poor bride needs passed appetizers, an open bar, and a Vera Wang dress. Stat! At least we have our priorities straight. When I get engaged (alevai!) and our families say they can't swing a huge wedding, I'll just ask them to take the money they would normally give to the poor and give it to us instead. Rabbi's orders.

Today's gemilut chasadim include more than just footing a wedding bill and attending a funeral. Community groups provide volunteer opportunities at after-school centers, women's shelters, and food pantries. They also run activity days with Jewish seniors who (bonus!) have nice Jewish grandsons. Volunteering at Shalom Village on Sunday could lead to a date with Al Rubin's grandson on Monday. God helps those who help others.

## TIKKUN OLAM

If gemilut chasadim is about lending a hand, then the third type of community service, *tikkun olam* (healing the world), is about having the whole world in your hands, your hopefully manicured hands. What? You can look good while doing good. Taken from a tale about gathering together sparks of God's light that scattered throughout the world, the phrase *tikkun olam* refers to uniting the world through mitzvot. Tackling issues like social justice, the environment, equality, and freedom, tikkun olam is community service that benefits the greater good on a global scale. It's all very "We Are the World."

# JOIN THE CLUB

So what'll it be today? Giving tzedakah, doing kind acts, healing the world, all of the above? There are scores of volunteer groups, and each one has its own take on community service. So choose one that champions an issue you feel passionate about—and attracts the kind of guys you'd like to get passionate with. Finding your community service match may take a few tries, so I suggest seeing several organizations before settling down with one. Here are a few to get you started:

### American Jewish World Service

AJWS is an international organization with a take-action attitude toward tikkun olam. Through advocacy, grant-making, and a traveling volunteer corps, this group fights hunger, poverty, and disease in populations around the world. They help put a roof over every head and an Empire chicken in every pot. With projects across Asia, Africa, and the Americas, AJWS gives volunteers a chance to roll up their sleeves and get their hands *schmutzidik* (dirty).

### Jewish Big Brothers and Big Sisters

Not quite ready to have a kid of your own? Then spend some time mentoring someone else's. This unique, one-on-one volunteer experience allows you to make a significant difference in one child's life. Through regularly scheduled field trips, meet-ups, and day-out adventures, you can mold your own mini-me. Plus, spending time with the little pisher is good practice for when you finally have your own challah in the oven.

### The American Israel Public Affairs Committee

Can you influence politics? Yes, you can. AIPAC is a pro-Israel lobbyist group. Members work with political leaders to champion policies that strengthen the U.S.-Israel relationship. Join your local chapter and schmooze with government directors, decision-makers, and a volunteer corps of politically minded men who look great in their power suits. Seriously, these handsome volunteers will rock your vote and your world.

### The Jewish Federation

Are you a yenta without a cause? The Jewish Federation will help you find one. The Federation is a powerhouse umbrella organization that oversees numerous nonprofit agencies and a large social-service network. With volunteer committees organized by industry (real estate, legal, entertainment, plus others) as well as demographic (young leadership, women's division, men's group, and more), J-Fed is a great way to get involved. Volunteer with literacy programs, Shabbat dinner deliveries, and community cleanup days. Organize fundraisers, coordinate food drives, and travel to Israel. Like an appetizer platter piled high with quesadillas, mozzarella sticks, and hot wings, the Federation serves up everything all in one place. Well, actually, they can't serve hot wings and quesadillas on the same tray; it wouldn't be kosher. So no hot wings, just hot volunteers.

## LADIES ONLY

Hot volunteers are important. But being active in the Jewish community is about more than meeting nice Jewish boys: it's also about meeting nice Jewish girls. Now that you're out of college, it can be challenging to meet other post-Bat Mitzvah, pre-babushka, fun-loving women. It'd be great to have a group of girlfriends who share your love of Judaism, your desire for community involvement, and your thirst for hard alcohol.

Equal parts philanthropy and socializing, Jewish women's groups are like sororities for adults—except you don't make T-shirts for every event or snap your fingers every time you agree. Also, there are fewer keg stands. But like SDT and AE Phi, group members form a cohesive sisterhood and create lifelong friendships. Bonding with Jewish women is an important way to bring Judaism into your life. Besides, what good is being a yenta if you don't have any one to gossip with?

## Hadassah

Hadassah, the Women's Zionist Organization of America, underwrites cutting-edge hospitals, progressive education, and Zionist youth programs in both Israel and the U.S. Founded in 1912, it now boasts more than 300,000 members, making it the largest women's organization in America. Thanks to an active Young Women's Division, Hadassah's mah-jongg tournaments, book clubs, and ladies' nights out aren't just for alter kockers. You can get pro-Israel with other young professionals.

## National Council of Jewish Women

A grassroots organization, the NCJW focuses on social justice for at-risk women, children, and families. They advocate for public policy issues like reproductive rights, workplace rights, and civil liberties. Local chapters boast lively Young Women's Councils and run unrivaled thrift shops, whose proceeds benefit their service programs. Even if you're too busy to be on a board, you're never too busy to shop. So in the least, hit up your local NCJW thrift store, and meet other young yentas while hunting for vintage Von Furstenberg.

## Jewish Women International

Founded in 1897, JWI (formerly B'nai Brith Women) focuses on breaking the cycle of domestic abuse and promotes safe homes, healthy relationships, and strong women. Meet other motivated girls, have a good time, and fight for a good cause. Well, don't fight, because their whole thing is antiviolence. So maybe just stand up for a good cause.

# RECREATIONAL ORGANIZATIONS

Volunteering is a great way to do the Jew thing. Not into helping others? How thoughtful of you. . . . No seriously, taking part in the Jewish community doesn't always have to be about doing something noble for the world, it can be about doing something nice for yourself. Sometimes, Jews just want to have fun.

## JEWISH SPORTS LEAGUES

"And now, starting at forward, a five-foot-two powerhouse from Chicago's North Shore, Caaarrrrrriiinn Daaavvviiisssss!" Okay, I'm not quite 5' 2" and I don't actually play basketball, but I could if I wanted to. From Dayton to D.C., Seattle to Miami, Jews everywhere are forming M.O.T.-only sports leagues. Whether you play basketball, football, or softball, there's a jersey out there with your Hebrew name on it. Organized through Jewish Community Centers (JCC), Jewish foundations, and ragtag groups of weekend warriors, these leagues allow you to relive the glory days of your college intramurals. If you're a more elite athlete, try out for the Maccabiah Games' open division. An international Olympic-style competition, this is your chance to bring home the gold and an athletic husband.

## CULTURE CLUB

All work and no play makes you a dull Jew. So take advantage of your city, and take your pupik someplace fresh. Open up your neighborhood's Jewish paper or your city's indie rag, and you'll discover all kinds of Jewish culture going down in your zip code. Take a photography class at the JCC, explore a new exhibit at a Jewish museum, or hear your favorite author speak at a Jewish book fair. Looking for something a little more innovative? KFAR Jewish Arts and JDub Records put together alternative programming for the next gen Jew. So catch klezmer punk, Jewish jazz fusion, and Israeli electronica at a club near you. Whether you're into frum-meets-funk or M.O.T.-meets-rock, these soulful, energetic concerts attract quite the crowd. These groups also sponsor Israeli films at the art house, Jewish improv at the black box, and major music festivals for Lag B'Omer, Chanukah, and Purim. Getting cultured will make you a more interesting catch and can help you catch more interesting men. So what are you waiting for? Shake a poulke. There are places to go and boys to see.

## JEWISH TRAVEL

Is vacation all you ever wanted? Well, not all you ever wanted, I'm sure you've also wanted things like a boyfriend, a promotion, and naturally blonde hair. But if a vacation is something you've ever wanted, pack your bags, baby; we're going to the Promised Land.

Taglit-Birthright Israel sends young Jewish adults (18–26) on a free, ten-day trip to Israel. There are no strings or tzitzit attached. Head to the homeland, strengthen your Jewish ties, and have a good time, all for a very good deal. Some things in life are free.

Now, you don't look a day older than twenty-six, but if your passport says otherwise, that's all right. You can still head to the Promised Land with promising other singles: you'll just have to pay for it. Through community groups like JNF and The Jewish Federation, or through private tour and travel companies, you can climb Masada, get a Dead Sea facial, and have a Tel Aviv hangover with other young M.O.T.s. And if you haven't had enough of doing the mitzvah thing, Livnot U'Lehibanot offers Israeli habitat for humanity-type journeys for Jews ages 21 to 42. And the best part of heading to the Land of Milk and Honey? There are a lot of honeys. Believe me, there are so many Jewboys within reach, you won't know where to flirt first.

Already been to Israel? You can still join the mile-chai club. Several private travel companies organize international vacations specifically for young Jewish professionals. Adventure awaits you in places like Aspen, Africa, Costa Rica, China, Brazil, and Peru. So pack your bags and your yarmulke; the world is your oyster—well, it would be if oysters weren't trayf.

# JEW YOUR OWN THING

Still haven't found what you're looking for? Don't really click with any Jewish cliques? Well, don't push a square peg through a frum hole. Rather than force-fit yourself into an established Jewish community group, just form a new one. Be a social entrepreneur. Abraham broke off and started his own club, and look how well that worked out for him.

## KOSHER WINE CLUB

There's more to life than Manischewitz. From Argentinean Bonardo to Spanish Tempranillo to my favorite, Bartenura's Italian Moscato, vineyards worldwide are fermenting quality kosher sauce. Your corner liquor store may not stock it next to the forties; but specialty wine shops, kosher grocers, and online wine Web sites carry kosher bottles ranging from $5 to $200. Each month choose a different grape, a different region, or take the Pepsi challenge and see how kosher varietals stand up to their no-ko counterparts. This one's oaky, this one's fruity, this one's schmaltzy.

## JEWISH BOOK CLUB

Take turns picking books written by Jewish authors or based on Jewish themes. I suggest you start with this one! But no pressure. . . .

## MOVIE MAVENS

Let's be honest, no one really reads for book club. So for this group, guests can just show up, watch movies, and play Ebert. Pick flicks with a Jewish theme or just a cute Jewish actor. Documentaries, comedies, dramas; it doesn't matter. If you serve up tasty apps, reduced-fat Orville Redenbachers, and a few cases of red wine, your friends will give the night four (Jewish) stars.

## TORAH AND TONIC

Looking to squeeze a little fun and inspiration out of the old Torah? Then combine your drinking with your davening—c'mon, all the cool kids are doing it. Host Torah-and-Tonic Shabbats, where your crew welcomes in the Sabbath with signature cocktails (pages 161-166) or hold Jew-and-Brew nights, where you recite a few blessings while throwing back a few beers. Start a Lox 'n' Learn brunch, where you learn about Moses while drinking MiMoshes, or form a happy holiday club, where the gang gets together for Tu B'Shevat wine tastings, Lag B'Omer barbeques, and Pizza in the (Sukkot) Hut. For a busy yenta like you, these Jews-and-Booze clubs are a fun way to stay connected to your friends and your heritage. Stay Jewish, San Diego.

## JEW FOOD CLUB

Bored with Judaism? Convert to Foodiasm. Start a club where friends whip up their family's famous version of a Jew food. Then get everyone together for—what else—essen and fressen! In April everyone fries matzah brei, in July you're all making tzimmes, and in September it's matzah ball soup. Or have each member cook one course of a potluck holiday meal. For Shavuot one friend cooks cheese knish, another brings cheese blintzes, and a third bakes strawberry cheesecake. And a fourth bakes cream-cheese brownies. And a fifth brings ice-cream cake. What? I'm sure somewhere the Talmud teaches us you can never have too many desserts. Have your guests bring copies of their recipes, so all you balabustas-in-training can make a few new noshes.

# EASY APRICOT KUGEL RECIPE

Make this dairy *lokshen* (noodle) kugel for your Foodiasm club, and you'll be the most popular girl in the community. All the women will want your recipe, and all the men will want you. And the best part? Cooking this kugel is as easy as boiling water and using a blender. But remember, a watched pot never boils ... and a watched boy never proposes. But a boy who eats this kugel might. Yes, it's that good!

## KUGEL

- 1 POUND BROAD EGG NOODLES
- 6 OUNCES CREAM CHEESE
- 2 CUPS APRICOT NECTAR
- ½ CUP MILK
- 2 STICKS (8 OUNCES) BUTTER, MELTED
- 1 CUP SUGAR
- 6 EGGS

## TOPPING

- 3 CUPS CRUSHED CORN FLAKES
- 5 TABLESPOONS GRANULATED SUGAR
- 1 TABLESPOON CINNAMON
- 2 STICKS (8 OUNCES) BUTTER, MELTED

Cook noodles in boiling water according to package directions. If it's already feeling too complicated, stop here, call your local deli for a kugel, and call it a day.

If you managed to boil the water, now's the time to drain the noodles.

Blend the cream cheese, apricot nectar, milk, butter, sugar, and eggs together in the blender.

Spread the noodles out in a greased 9 x 13-inch baking pan. Pour the apricot mixture over it and stir slightly.

In a separate bowl, mix the corn flakes, sugar, cinnamon, and butter to combine, then spread the topping evenly over the entire dish. Bake for 1 hour at 350°F. While your kugel's cooking, run upstairs to shower, get dressed, and do your hair. Remove kugel from the oven, let sit for thirty minutes, and impress your guests with your good cooking and your great looks.

**TIPS:**

• This kugel can be cooked in advance and reheated in the oven for a few minutes at 325°F. While reheating, cover with aluminum foil so the topping doesn't get *farbrent* (burnt).

• This kugel tastes great cold, so leftovers can be eaten straight from your fridge. And anything eaten while standing at the fridge doesn't count toward your day's calorie total. Everyone knows snacking while standing is guilt-free. Besides, this has apricot nectar, so it must be healthy. . . .

# CHAPTER 5

# PUT A LID ON IT
## (HEADCOVERINGS)

After dinner and a movie, and a drink, and another drink, Matt and I are standing awkwardly on my stoop. This is the telltale moment. Are we making small talk, or are we making out? He grabs my waist, pulls me closer, and . . . starts talking. Just kidding, who could just talk with a shayna punim like mine? Matt closes his eyes, leans in, and kisses me. Or at least tries to.

Every culture has its own signature make-out move. The French touch tongues. The Eskimo touch noses. And the Jews touch . . . hair. You heard me. Hair. If two big-haired Jews go in for a first kiss and don't execute the proper head tilt, their Jewfros lock before their lips do.

So Matt and I are looking at a giant Jewfro mash-up. My Moses mop falls in his face, his kosher curls hit my head; it's all kinds of ugly. I try to caress his cheek with one hand and hold my Heeb hair back with the other, but that totally throws me off balance. And while my tongue never makes it in his mouth, a strand of my curls do. Based on his expression, my shampoo may smell like passionfruit, but it tastes like drek. Great. If this is what happens when we try to kiss, what's going to happen when we start stuffing kishke? I'm doomed.

It's a disaster. It's not fair. Why does this hair always happen to me?

It's not a new dilemma. As a kid, I quickly realized that the girls in fairy tales all had long, straight, blond strands. They got glass stilettos, a superhot prince, and good hair days? No wonder they lived happily ever after. What if I get Rapunzeled? I can't let down my hair. It doesn't grow long: it grows out. Which would be great if my prince was across the river and needed a sturdy bridge, but if he's seven stories below, I've got nothing. Nada. Gornisht. He's moving on to Goldilocks, and I'm still stuck here in the singles' tower.

My 'tween years were no better. Seventh grade was plain awful. I had Bat Mitzvahs every weekend and frizz head every day. I just wanted to fit in, but I didn't look like all the other girls in my class. Are you there, God? It's me, Carin. Forget increasing my bust; how about decreasing my 'do?

Then in high school, I'd wait by the phone, but it didn't matter if he called. I couldn't hold the phone up to my head. There was a good four inches of 'fro between my ear and the receiver. Who could hear if he was asking me out?

My love life still suffers today. My dates don't let me ride shotgun, because my big keppe creates a blind spot. At restaurants we have to wait for a table for three—me, my date, and my hair. For some reason, I don't think that's what he meant by a threesome. And when a guy says he wants a woman with curves, he's not talking about her hair. He might be down with tousled waves or that crazy bed-head look. But when he picks you up for a date, he wants your hair to fit through the door. Guess size does matter.

My hair is in a constant state of disaster. As is my love life. Let's say Matt gets past my Heeb hair and we actually start dating. What happens when things get serious and I start crashing at his place? He might give me half a drawer for my clothes. But he's not going to give me a whole medicine cabinet for my products. And we can't possibly go away for a weekend together. I can't take this 'fro on the road. How would I explain lugging along my giant suitcase of serum? Guys like girls who carry-on. In the luggage sense, not the rambling sense. Great, another strike against me.

So that's it. Big hair isn't just a pain in the tuchus to style, it's a romantic liability. Especially if you're dating other Jews. Saturday night's main event? 'Fro vs. 'Fro.

Wait—that's it! Why am I making myself meshuggene? I'm not alone in this. My hair's not hitting forehead; it's meeting mane. Matt's mane. My nice Jewish boy has a big Jewish 'fro. His hair is large. Huge. Venti. So who's he to judge?

I decide to rerelease my curls on Matt, hoping he's up for a game of bumper hair. He's not up for it, down with it, or into it. He pulls away from our kiss, mumbles something about me looking like an original member of Poison, and runs to his car. The night's ruined. And so are my chances of becoming Mrs. Matt Schwartz. Or would I be Mrs. Carin Schwartz? Or Carin Davis-Schwartz? Or—whatever, a bad date by any other name still stinks.

The thing is my date with Matt was bad because of him, not my hair. I've got gorgeous hair, and any man would be lucky to run his fingers through it—without getting them caught. Look, I'm not saying I'm never reaching for the Frizz-Ease again, but I'm going to start feeling more confident about my locks. And my looks. And if Matt doesn't like it when I go with the 'fro, then I'll find someone else who does. I'll find someone better. I'll find myself a mensch. Then I'm going to wash that Matt right out of my hair.

## KEEP IT UNDER YOUR KIPPAH

I'm not the only Jew to have hair trouble. The Jewfro's been with us since the beginning. You think Adam and Eve's only punishment was expulsion from Eden? Nope, God also handed us big hair. Luckily, the ancient rabbis recognized this issue early on and gave us an easy out. Why do you think Jews are always covering their heads? The rabbis knew it was the only way to keep our hair in check. Of course, covering one's noggin isn't actually mentioned in the Torah, so there's no real way of knowing how the tradition started. My hair-hiding theory isn't the only one out there.

Some Jews believe it all goes back to ancient Rome, when servants covered their heads and free men didn't. To show they were servants of God, Jews began to cover their heads while studying, praying, or reciting a blessing. It was an outpouring of reverence and R-E-S-P-E-C-T for the big guy. Eventually some

Jews weren't down with the whole servant thing and covered their heads simply as an acknowledgment that God is above us. A higher power is always there. Now . . . and still now . . . still up there.

Others argue that wearing a kippah is like tying a string around your head; it's a constant reminder to make everyday acts holy. Keeping kosher elevates eating to a higher plateau, and wearing a kippah lifts living to a new level. It reminds you to be all that you can be. All the time.

Still some say that like a Jewish Varsity jacket, a kippah lets everyone know you're on the team. Ancient Jewish leaders tried to slow assimilation between Jews and their neighboring communities. Covering one's dome was a uniquely Jewish fashion statement that gave Jews a sense of community and identity. Today many Jews view kippot not just as a symbol of piety, but as a show of their stanch Jewish pride. In a post-Holocaust world, they like to exercise their freedom to the let the world know they're Jewish. Plus, they like to hide their bald spots.

Now, the head covering custom isn't kept across the board. While Orthodox Jews cover up at all times, many Conservative Jews only take cover in synagogue and during holy times, and most Reform congregations (who once forbid kippot) now have a personal choice policy. It's never required, wear it when you like. Or not.

## THE CUTTING EDGE

While observant men keep their heads covered, they have no problem sporting full facial hair. Why the double standard? Beards make rabbis look wise. Plus the Torah says a man shouldn't use a straight edge or knife to cut the corners of his head. Corners? Personally, I don't know many blockheads, but let's just go with it and say that's why observant Jews grow year-round beards and *pe'ot* (side curls). Thanks to a loophole, many modern Jews skip the ZZ Top look and just use electric razors (with a scissors action). I find a man with a little stubble more than a little sexy, so I'm down with this practice. Let's give praise for that sexy three-day shadow! Hallelujah.

# MEN'S HEADGEAR

Frum Frisbee, Pious Pancake, Baruch Beanie. Yup, kids, today we're going to talk about yarmulkes, that small disk that sits atop many—but not all—a Jewfro. Sure, most men choose to sport a kippah, but there's no significance behind its 360 shape. Unlike a round challah, the round disc doesn't mark the beginning of one thing, the end of the other. It doesn't symbolize it's a small world, or we're all one big happy world, or the world was created in seven days. It's just a conveniently shaped beanie that's become a fashion statement. When it comes to Jewish headgear, what's important is that you cover your head, not what you cover it with. If it conceals your keppe, it's all good. That's why Jews can choose from a full line of headgear. Let's see what the designers are premiering in the men's fall collection:

**KIPPAH**: There's no difference between a kippah and a yarmulke. Kippah is Hebrew and yarmulke is Yiddish. No matter what you call it, the little black beanie is a wardrobe staple; it goes with everything and is appropriate for any occasion. Kippot also come in suede, cotton, silk, velvet, embroidered with team logos, covered with cartoon characters, and, of course, engraved with the names of brides and grooms. While I highly doubt anyone received an "Abraham & Sarah" wedding kippah, this modern phenomenon is a nice way to commemorate a simcha and saves you from having to spill big bucks to buy your own beanie. That in turn allows you to spend more money on some ridiculous waffle maker that your friends registered for and will never use.

**BUKHARIN KIPPAH**: Originally worn by the Jews of Central Asia, this colorful cylinder sits two to three inches high and has become quite the rage with young men in America. I'm not sure if that's because of its exotic, colorful design or the fact that it makes short Jewish men look two inches taller.

**BLACK HAT**: Some believe the black hat tradition started when

European rulers forced Jews to wear black; others think the black symbolizes the serious nature with which many Orthodox Jews view their religion. I think black is always in fashion. Ask Angelina Jolie, she always wears black. Not that she's a Jew. But she might adopt one.

**BASEBALL HAT**: An irreverent way to show reverence, this look is popular with the younger set. Casual and athletic, this understated approach is a chill alternative to the good old skullcap. Most often worn outside of formal services, it's a great way for a man to show loyalty to God and his hometown team. Go, Cubs! Go, God!

# WOMEN'S HEADGEAR

Many Jewish women cover their heads during services for the same reasons men do. What's good for the goose is good for the gander. Not that anyone uses the word *gander* anymore. If you're going to refer to women as poultry, the kids today are going with "chicks."

Married orthodox women go deep undercover and hide their hair all day every day in the name of *tzniut* (modesty). Observant Jews believe a woman's hair is so sexy she needs to conceal it from any man who isn't her husband. Think: "I'm too sexy for my hair . . ."

Like jewelry, purses, and bedazzled cell phone covers, women's headcoverings come in all colors, shapes, and styles:

**KIPPAH**: Like adding the names of the *Imahot* (Rachel, Sarah, Rebecca, and Leah) whenever we mention the *Avot* (Abe, Isaac, and Jake), wearing a kippah can be a conscious statement of egalitarian Judaism. It's all very "You go, girl."

**LACE DOILY**: This lace disk resembles the paper doily grade school students use to make homemade Valentines. Some women wear the doily flat, others fold it in half, and still others go for the quartered look. No matter how you fold it, the doily is a fashion nightmare.

We've taken leaps with low-rise jeans, gut-sucking Spanx, and push-up bras, but we're still sporting napkins on our heads. Oy vey iz mir!

**HAT**: The art of hats may have been lost with Jackie O, but the pill box, the bandeau, and the cloche are all making comebacks at congregations worldwide.

**SHEITELS (WIGS)**: For the woman who always covers her hair but still wants to look like she has hair.

**TIECHELS (SCARVES)**: Available in every color and fabric, tying your hair up bandanna-style is an easy way to pull your outfit together while keeping a lid on it.

**SNOOD**: A pre-tied, elasticized scarf or bandanna, the snood is choice of the busy Jewish woman. Like canned soup, cake mixes, and jarred gefilte fish, the snood is a handy shortcut for the woman who hasn't got time to waste.

**THE BABUSHKA**: Popular with bubbes everywhere, this scarf tied under the chin is off-limits to anyone under 80. I ban you from it. It's dead to you.

# LET YOUR HAIR DOWN

Any Jewish girl who doesn't cover her hair has fallen victim to a major hair crisis.

Murphy's Law—actually Murphy probably wasn't Jewish, so let's go with Moishe's Law—says that you never have good hair when you need it. Good hair happens when you've got no place to go. Take it from a girl who once ordered in a pizza just so some guy, any guy, even just the Domino's delivery guy, witnessed my good hair day.

I know, thou shall not covet thy neighbor's hair, but it's not easy sporting a Jewfro. And styling it? Like Jacob wrestling with the angel. What's a Jew to do? Anything but panic. So you're hitting the town with a hottie. You don't need a Moses-sized miracle to get your Jewfro looking date-worthy; you just need a few good moves.

## THE GIRL WITH THE CURL

Big is beautiful, so flaunt your curls, if not on the first date, then on the second, or the third. At some point you gotta go big or go home. But going big doesn't mean you need to look bad. Follow these tips and you won't have a frizzy hair out of place:

- Like to throw back a few martinis? Well, you're not the only one who needs a drink. Hydrate your hair! Moisture prevents the fly-aways that make curls look frizzy. So trade in your discount products for some salon-quality, extra-moisturizing shampoo and conditioner. Like switching from well drinks to top shelf, it'll cost you a few more dollars, but you'll thank me in the morning. Not that you'll wake up next to your date in the morning, but if you do—well, the shampoo's working for you.
- Brushes are the bad boys of styling tools, so stay away. They strip the curl and lead to all kinds of static. Instead, run your fingers or a wide-toothed comb through your wet hair—once. The more you touch, the more you frizz. So make like a nice Jewish boy and keep your hands off.
- Vigorously towel-drying your hair will make the curls go every-where. So save your aggressive moves for after dinner and let your hair air-dry.
- Still not getting that "Don't hate me because I'm beautiful" look? Twirl small sections of wet hair around your finger, clip them up, and then let them dry completely. Unpin the twists and shake the curls loose. This trick works really well with long, wavy hair. No,

you're not too old for long hair. Whoever wrote that women over thirty can't have long hair also wrote that women over thirty can't get schtupped. Yeah, right. My guidebook can beat up her guidebook any day.

- Product is a girl's best friend. To get neat, bouncy curls, schpritz shaping products (curl activator or booster) when your hair is wet and use refining products (antifrizz serum or curl reviver) once it's dry. But remember, when getting ready for a date, use just enough goo to achieve the look you want. Don't overdose. Sticky, stiff hair is never good. Let him be the stiff one.

- Hit the beach. The saltwater makes your curls stick together. So grab a book, some SPF, and get your hot bod to the ocean. If you're in Israel, get your big hair to the Dead Sea now. Who cares that you can float there? You can have good hair there!

- Switch your zip code. Humidity causes hair to frizz; so get to a dry, hot climate. It's no accident that the Jews wandered the desert for forty years. They weren't lost; they were just enjoying four decades of good hair.

## PLAYING IT STRAIGHT

You have to embrace your curls. But every so often there's something about shiny straight hair that makes you feel sexy. It might be the way men always say, "Wow, your hair looks sexy." Here are two ways to get things straight:

**FLAT IRON**: A must-have for the modern Jewess, these lifesavers are sold at your friendly neighborhood beauty supply. If you have a hot date, wash your hair the day before and flat-iron it the day of. Not only does your hair take to the straight better, but it saves you valuable first-date prep time, so you can do things like shave your legs and down a shot.

**HAIR SALON BLOWOUT**: This surefire solution for runaway hair takes all the stress out of the situation. But it may also take all the money out of your fake Kate Spade, so I suggest saving this luxury for a special occasion or a major hair emergency.

........................................................................

# SAMSON

You can't talk Jewfro without talking Samson. An angel told Sam's barren mom she would have a son, but he must never cut his hair. It would mark his devotion to God and be the source of his strength.

Samson grew to be a mighty man, a circumcised Hercules. He killed lions with his bare hands, defended the Israelites from the Philistines, and became a great judge. But like most men, Sam couldn't keep his mind out of his pants. He had it bad for a sexy Philistine named Delilah. The Philistines bribed Delilah to ask Sammy his secret. Twice he lied to her, but the third time she begged, and probably threatened to withhold sex, and he caved. Delilah cut Sam's hair; Sam lost his strength and was thrown in jail. With time Sam's hair grew back, and he asked God to return his strength. Strong again, our Jewish Fabio broke out of jail, killed a couple thousand Philistines, and died a hero.

Okay, so what can we take from this oh-so-uplifting tale of love and hair?

- Even the strongest man is weak when it comes to women.
- With good hair comes great power. One bad trim and you could lose it all. So when talking cut and color, listen to your hairdresser . . . or at least to God.
- Samson lost his strength by breaking his vow with God. He regained his strength by asking God for help.

So what's hair got to do with it? Not much. Story's moral: success is not based on hair alone. So if your Jewfro is out of control, no worries. Just be your witty, sexy self, and your date should go well. But just in case, maybe give a quick shout-out to God on your way to the restaurant.

# PLAY IT BY HAIR

It may be a small world, but you've got big hair. You're not alone. Heeb hair comes in all shapes, sizes, and heights. Check out these famous Jew 'dos.

**ABRA CADABFRO**—David Copperfield and David Blaine

**BALD WITH A SIDE OF FRO**—Larry David and Jason Alexander

**BED HEAD**—Dr. Ruth Westheimer

**BROADWAY DANNY FROS**—Woody Allen

**CHICK SCHTICK**—Sarah Silverman

**COPAFROBANA**—Barry Manilow

**COUNTING FROS**—Adam Duritz

**CURLS! ALL I REALLY WANT IS CURLS!**—The Beastie Boys

**D'OH FRO**—Krusty the Clown

**ENCINO MANE**—Pauly Shore

**E.T. FRO HOME**—Steven Spielberg

**FULL METAL FRO**—Gene Simmons

**FUNNY CURL**—Barbra Streisand

**HAIR BAND HEEB**—David Lee Roth

**HAIRY BRADSHAW**—Sarah Jessica Parker

**HIP-HOP HAIR**—Matisyahu

**LIKE FATHER, LIKE FRO**—Jerry Stiller and Ben Stiller

**MEADOW "THE FRO" SOPRANO**— Jamie-Lynn Sigler

**MEET THE FROKERS**—Dustin Hoffman

**OUTRAGEOUS FROTUNE**—Bette Midler

**PIG TAILS OF A FOURTH GRADE NOTHING**—Judy Blume

**RAISING HAIRIZONA**—Joel and Ethan Cohen

**RELATIVELY LARGE FRO**—Albert Einstein

**ROCK-AND-ROLL HIGH SHUL**—Joey Ramone

**ROSEANNE FROSEANNADANNA**—Gilda Radner

**SAVED BY THE FRO**—Dustin Diamond and Elizabeth Berkley

**SCARBOROUGH HAIR**—Paul Simon and Art Garfunkel

**SWEET HAIR-O-LINE**—Neil Diamond

**TENACIOUS 'DO**—Jack Black

**THREE STOOGE 'DO**—Larry Fine, Moe Howard, and Curly Howard

**@#$%&ING FRO**—Howard Stern

**TO BOLDLY FRO WHERE NO MAN HAS GONE BEFORE**—
   Leonard Nimoy and William Shatner

**TRANSFROMERS**—Shia LaBeouf

**UPTOWN CURL**— Billy Joel

**YOUNG FROKENSTEIN**—Gene Wilder

**WELCOME BACK, KOSHER**—Gabe Kapler

**WHAT'S THE DEAL WITH BIG HAIR?**—Jerry Seinfeld

**WHEN HAIRY MET SALLY**—Billy Crystal

# CHAPTER 6

# ARE YOU MY MENSCH?
## (DATING)

Who's to say how you'll meet your mensch? Who by water and who by fire? Who by online and who in person? Who by setup and who by pickup? Who the heck knows—so when my friends decide to host a giant Jewish wingman party, I'm in! Everyone has to bring a single friend of the opposite sex who they either unsuccessfully dated or could never dream of dating. It's like a potluck dinner with leftover dates. It's like a clothing swap with hand-me-down hotties. Sure, the idea of recycling someone's romantic castaway is a little cockamamie. But know all those other fish in the sea? Someone reeled them in and tossed them back; so now it's my turn to go-fish. I throw on a low-cut shirt, a high-cut skirt, and head out to catch a mensch.

My wingman, Marc, and I arrive around eight, and the party's already packed. It's a who's who of L.A. Jews—Westside surfers, downtown lawyers, Hollywood hipsters. Forget what four out of five doctors recommend: four out of five doctors are here. With all these Jews to choose from, what's a girl to do but hit the ground running? Well, technically I start running, trip in my heels, and fall flat to the ground. But I don't think anyone noticed, do you? I pick myself up, pretend that spilled vodka isn't mine, and set off on my manhunt. That's when I run into Jason. He drops his cell, I drop my jaw. Two years ago Jason and I met through our mutual friend Melissa. For the next six months we had an on-again, off-again, on-me-again relationship. One day he pulled an Elijah and just disappeared. I haven't seen him since. Well, someone call VH1, I know where he is now. He's Melissa's wingman.

"Jason, um, hey, er, hi. How've you been? I, um, well, uh, gotta go, bye!"

That was fun. Hoping to meet someone whose bris I can't personally confirm, I take a quick lap around the lounge. I can't believe all these guys are up for grabs—or up for grabbing, depending how the night goes. And the best part? Everyone's prescreened. They all play wingman to one of my friends—the Goose to her Maverick, the Aaron to her Moses, the kasha to her varnishkes. These guys have my girls' backs . . . and they have cute backsides. Except for that one—

Wait, I know that one—that's Gabe. Talk about ghosts of blind dates past, my friend Shana set us up last summer. For our date Gabe suggested we rent bikes by the beach . . . then showed up wearing nothing but shorts. No shirt, no shoes, not sexy. I haven't seen Gabe or his chest rug since. But tonight he's Shana's wingman.

"Gabe, hey, you look nice, a shirt's a good look for you. . . ."

Eager to find a less awkward scene, I make a beeline for the bar—big mistake. I see my blind date from three years ago, my setup from six months ago, and my date to my freshman AE Phi semi-formal. And believe me, that ex didn't mark the spot. But wonder of wonder, miracle of miracles, like every other Jewboy I've ever been set up with, he's here tonight. Are you kidding me with the run-ins? The only ex who isn't here is my date to the third-grade Purim carnival. Oh wait, there he is. . . .

I thought a wingman party would be the perfect place to find a new guy. Well wrench, meet plans. I'm not getting to know new men; I'm just running into men I already know. Apparently my friends already fixed me up with their wingmen, and now I'm double-dipping in the dating pool. Yes, this party boasts dozens of Jewish bachelors, but I've dated them all before. And talk about Jewish geography—of all the Jew joints, in all the towns, in all the world, they all walked into mine. Which is my clue to walk out.

But where in the world's my wingman, Marc? In the corner kissing Rob Stein's wing-girl. Guess one man's trash is another man's treasure, or in this case, pleasure. Looks like this cockamamie wingman thing worked out for one of us.

And while my night didn't end in a love connection, it could have been worse. Okay, fine, there's no way my night could have been worse, but it definitely could have been better. And it's that possibility that keeps me coming back. Sure, finding your beshert at a wingman party would be odd, but my friends have met their hubs in really random ways: at a shiva house, on a mountaintop, and having a one-night stand that's now lasted seven years. Why is this night different than all other nights? Because tonight might be the night you meet your man. So put down the Cabernet, get off your couch, and Carpe Diem! Seize the date! RSVP yes to that Federation mixer, show your punim at a singles' Shabbat, and get your pupik to a wingman party. You never know: someone's wingman for the night could be your copilot for life. And I, for one, am ready for takeoff.

## LOOKING FOR A MENSCH IN A HAYSTACK

Blind dates, wing dates, coffee dates, drink dates, first dates, JDates, SpeedDates, day dates—sometimes Jewish dating feels a lot like dancing the Hora: you just keep going in circles. But eventually the room will stop spinning. Unless you keep pounding the Baron Herzog, then the spinning continues. But the dating? It may seem like you're getting nowhere, but every failed fix-up and dead-end flirt moves you one step closer to meeting your mate. So you just have to keep trying. You think Joshua gave up when Jericho's walls didn't fall? No, he circled that city six more times. You think Moses gave up when Pharaoh said no to letting us go? That took ten tries. You think God gave up after creating men?

Nope, he went back to the drawing board and got it right with women. Point is, Jews never give up and we never complain. Okay, so we complain a lot while we're not giving up. But still, we just keep going. And so should you.

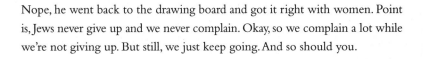

# IT'S BESHERT

It's true. To find your Jewish prince, you have to kiss a lot of frogs . . . and nudniks and zhlubs. And nuchschlepers, schlimazels, and schmendriks. And don't forget, no-goodniks, schmucks, and schnorrers. Plus that one guy Kenny, who was just plain weird. You've kissed them all. You still haven't found who you're looking for—your beshert.

My beWhat? Before we're born, God picks a *beshert* (meant to be) for each of us. That's right, we each have a match literally made in heaven. I have soul mate, you have a soul mate, we all have soul mates. God's made sure of that. Thanks, Big Guy. But then why am I running around dating every dreykop, nebbish, and shmegegge to ever hit the Jewish singles' scene? Couldn't God just tell me who my beshert is? Why not drop me an e-mail?

I know, I know, God makes the match but gives us the free will to find each other. Well, how about a little less free will, so I could have a little more free time? Would that be so hard? How many hours have I spent over the years trawling the bars, surviving bad blind dates, and dating insignificant others? If I hadn't wasted all that time looking for my beshert, I could have been a contender. I could have earned a Ph.D. or cured cancer or written the great Jewish-American novel. And its sequel. My life would have been so different if I only had the 411 on my beloved.

# COME OUT, COME OUT, WHEREVER YOU ARE

Instead, I have no idea where my future husband is. Thanks to the boyfriend protection program, he could be anywhere. So I keep searching and searching and searching. Sometimes I feel like that little bird looking for his mother: I go from date to date to date asking, "Are you my mensch?"

"No, I'm a cow," said Jim, who had the appetite of a college boy, but not the body.

"No, I'm a dog," said Joe, who kissed my friend—and me—at the same party.

"Of course not, I'm a steam shovel," said Frank, who was shoveling a lot of stuff. . . .

I've been looking for my match since the first slow-dance at my Bat Mitzvah. I don't know where else to look, I don't know what else to do. Like a bagel during Passover, he's nowhere to be found. So I ask for a little help from my friends. And my mother. And the shul yenta. And even you—yes, you reading this book—do you know a nice Jewish boy looking for a short, saucy girl? Your cousin, Stu? Sure, I'll meet him for drinks, why not? When you're looking to get a ring, leave no rock unturned and no setup unaccepted.

## MATCHMAKER, MATCHMAKER, MAKE ME A MATCH ALREADY

The blind date is a Jewish tradition as old as Judaism itself. Our patriarch, Isaac, didn't pick up his wife Rebecca at a local bar or meet her at the Sukkot harvest dance. His father, Abraham, asked his buddy, Eliezer, to make a match. Eliezer saw Becky at a well, thought she'd be perfect for Ike, and fixed up those two crazy kids. Ike and Becky not only got married but helped found a religion . . . your religion. Guess that fix-up worked out well for them and for you. After-school lesson learned? Never say no to a blind date.

Ever since then *shadchans* (matchmakers) have played a big role in bringing Jews together. That's almost 4,000 years of yentas nudzhing, "Have I got a guy for you!" Today, many Orthodox communities still call upon a professional shadchan to pair up their single sons and daughters. The matchmaker does all the groundwork and identifies eligible Jews with similar values, observances, and goals. The one goal all shadchan clients share is marriage. By hiring a pro, singletons in a hurry to the chuppah can weed out anyone looking to keep things casual. These Jews are flirting for keeps.

Now, matchmakers don't have to be trained professionals; your friends, co-workers, and even mothers can try this at home. Anyone can make a *shidduch* (match) and believe me, they all want to. Most Jews know plenty of single Jews, and nothing would give them more *naches* (joy) than bringing you together. You just need to toot your own shofar and let everyone know you're looking. You'll instantly have a minyan of men to meet. And different from the bachelors you pick up at bars, these boychiks come recommended. Recommended by your Great-Aunt Mollie's next-door neighbor, Saul, but nonetheless, recommended.

# WWW.GETMETOTHECHUPPAH.COM

Internet dating sites are basically cyber-shadchans. They help you sift through potential dates and pinpoint the men who have successful careers, dynamic personalities, and chiseled abs. Well, they would if anyone ever filled out their profile honestly.

Whether you want a hot-buttered frum, a boychik next door, or a slick city macher, they're all online. From JDate to Frumster to SawYouAtSinai, there are dozens of Jewish dating sites, and they all boast matches that have led to marriage. The key to finding your true love online is—no, not writing a good profile—posting the perfect picture. It should scream "Beam me up, hottie!"

But the written portion of the test is key, too. When crafting your personal profile, don't just describe yourself: sell yourself. This is your chance to charm the tallis off that suitor, to make him laugh his tuchus off. If a man finds your profile witty, survey says he'll write you. So be snappy, be sexy, and above all else, give good flirt. Here are a few tips to help you turn a few keppes:

- **If you're going to talk kashrut, be clever. Writing "I keep kosher" won't captivate anyone. Let the J-boys know that you're down for separate dishes, but you're up for having fun. Try saying "I'm a beer-drinking, mensch-seeking, Hebrew hottie who knows her way around a kosher kitchen, a glatt grocery, and a downtown dive bar."**

- Don't be just another candle in the menorah. Make like the shamas and stand out. To distinguish yourself from ChallahBackGirl18 and SuperYenta5, be specific. Rich details will help him remember you. Try replacing "I like to work out" with "I was the MVP of my kindergarten tee ball team, I played intramural soccer at Northwestern, and I currently keep my cute tush in shape by running 10Ks." Now your potential date knows that you're athletic, you graduated from a top school, and you can still rock a pair of running shorts. In fact, he's picturing your cute tush in them right now.

- A little kibbitz goes a long way. So while every J-girl out there will say "I'm as comfortable in a T-shirt and jeans as I am in a dress," a knockout M.O.T. like you should say "I'm as comfortable in a tank top and Sox hat as I am in a strapless dress and heels. But I'm more comfortable when I take them all off." Remember your profile isn't just some form to fill out; it's your opportunity to cyber-flirt. You want to work it, work it, own it. . . .

- Looking for someone special to spend Shabbat with? Writing "I like to make Shabbat dinner" won't whet anyone's appetite. Instead, show the guys online you're a dynamic girl who's looking to mix her Jewish roots with her happening lifestyle. Try something like: "I'm looking for a guy who enjoys a good challah and a good time, who's always up for making Shabbat dinner and doing the double mitzvah."

## MY ONLINE PROFILE

Because you're a trusted reader, I'm going to share my personal JDate profile with you. It's not perfect, but it's effective. I had an inbox filled with messages and a whole tribe of *N.J.B.s* (nice Jewish boys) asking me out.

**DESCRIBE MYSELF:** I'm an Internet dating virgin. So I've never shopped online for a date before—not that there's anything wrong with that. I've never done J-Chemistry or J-Onenightstand, but I thought it was time I threw my Cubs hat in the ring. I'd describe myself as a *Sports Illustrated* swimsuit model meets Nobel Prize winner. Well, if SI had 5' 2" centerfolds, and they gave a Nobel Prize for talking. Other noteworthy skills include making a mean kugel, supplying sarcastic remarks, and giving good conversation. On Saturdays I can be found hiking in the hills, reading on the beach, or grabbing margaritas with friends. On any given Sunday, I can be found watching my Chicago Bears, teaching Hebrew school, or enjoying the sunshiny day. I've also been know to spend quality couch time with *The Office*, the Food Network, and whatever '80s movie TBS has running on a loop. Originally from Chicago, I went to UCLA and have been cheering on my Bruins ever since. So my turn-ons include deep-dish pizza and basketball tickets. If you're not quick on the uptake and don't get my pop culture references, you are not the droid I am looking for. I'm close with my brothers, I'm a little bit silly, and yes, my picture was taken recently. Résumé, college transcript, letters of recommendation, junior-high report card, and second-grade paper on Herbert Hoover available upon request.

**MY IDEAL FIRST DATE:** Leaves me smiling as I drive home and has me checking my e-mail constantly the next day, hoping he writes.

**MY IDEAL RELATIONSHIP:** Both people risk opening their hearts fully. So even everyday moments, like watching TV or making late-night grilled cheese together, are filled with laughter and love. My boyfriend will be my best friend and my biggest fan.

**MY PAST RELATIONSHIPS**: Let's see, my first kiss was on the lawn at overnight camp the night of the masquerade ball. My first breakup was on the lawn at overnight camp two days after the masquerade ball. And yes, I've gotten better at kissing since then.

**MY IDEAL MATCH:** A smart, sharp, witty, funny, driven, giving, caring, open guy who makes my heart smile. And a cute tush is never frowned upon.

# AT LAST, WE MEET FACE TO FACE

You've been online and you've come up with bupkes. No boyfriend, no relationship, no ring. Now what? Now, your mission, if you choose to accept, is to find The One in person.

I accept, I accept. I accept the mission, I'll accept the proposal, I'm ready to accept it all. But we all know meeting a man in person is more than a *Mission: Impossible*—it's a *Mission: Farkakte*. It's a never-ending cycle of getting your hopes up, getting your hair done, and getting turned down. But you have no choice. Sure, online dating is essential, but you can't just sit at home waiting for the perfect man to fall into your laptop. Dating is a full-contact sport. So get off your tush and go where the Jewish boys are.

## SINGLED OUT

Dedicating a whole night to a date you instantly know you're not interested in is a waste of time and a good hair day. And who has time to waste when your matrimonial clock is ticking? So get yourself to an organized Jewish singles' night. These super-sized events are like the Costco of dating—you can shop for your beshert in bulk. You can meet a baker's dozen of nice Jewish boys; you can knock out ten JDates at once. Why take it one date at a time when you can weed through a ton in one night?

Just grab a girlfriend and brave those singles' picnics and potlucks. Buy a ticket to the Spring Jew-bilee and the Shushan Shindig. Another can't-miss? The massive Jewish singles' balls held on Christmas Eve. The Matzo Ball, Knishmas, The Vodka Latke—you should show your shayna punim at all of them. Yes, sometimes these giant Jew-o-ramas can feel a little contrived, and you might think they make you look a little desperate. But just remember, everyone there is in the same boat as you. In this case, Noah's ark.

# I FEEL THE NEED, THE NEED FOR SPEED

Most Jewish singles events don't try to Splenda-coat it; they're direct and to the point. If you're here, you're looking. And nothing is more direct than SpeedDating. This national fast-talking phenomenon was created by a Los Angeles rabbi in 1998. It makes sense that SpeedDating started as a Jew thing, between the daveners and the yentas we're all well-trained to talk ten miles a minute.

# LOCATION, LOCATION, LOCATION

Been there, done him? Then go someplace else. I know girls who have snagged their guy standing in the kosher wine section of a gourmet liquor store, swimming laps at the Jewish Community Center (JCC) pool, and grabbing lunch at a kosher pizza pub. Story's moral: if you want to meet a Jewish man, get your pupik to a Jewish hub.

Don't just run to the grocery store: stop by the kosher market. Don't buy prepackaged turkey slices; hit up the kosher butcher. Don't schvitz in front of just anyone, work out at the JCC. Get your wedding gifts at a Judaica shop, buy your books at a Jewish bookstore, and make reservations at a kosher restaurant. I can't guarantee you'll meet a man while waiting for a table at a kosher café. But if you do, you'll know he meets your mohel-only requirement. And if you don't, well, at least you got to nosh on some good kosher grub.

# JUST SAY YES

It's dating 101—accept any invitation to a Jewish event. You never know when someone's invited their single co-worker, old college buddy, or cute bachelor cousin to come along. If a friend invites you to a Shabbat dinner party, say yes. If a co-worker invites you to his Passover Seder, say yes. If a colleague invites you to her son's bris, say yes, yes, yes. There's nothing wrong with flirting over a little lost foreskin.

## JUST SHOW UP

All faputzed and no place to go? You have no excuse. If you belong to a synagogue, actually go to the young adult events. If you're a member of a community service group, try actually attending the meetings and volunteer events. And then double-up and attend a fundraiser for a friend's nonprofit. I know the ticket to the (dance, banquet, poker game, insert generic Jewish fundraiser here) is expensive, but that means any man you meet there was either born with a fleishig spoon in his mouth or earns enough to cover the cost.

## ALUMNI ASSOCIATION

Get back to your roots. No, not the brunette ones that grow in under your highlights; the ones you planted throughout your adolescence. Did you belong to a Jewish youth group? Attend a Jewish summer camp? Take a Birthright trip to Israel? Jewish youth organizations all have active alumni associations that offer packed event calendars. Get listed with Project Reconnect (USY, Camp Ramah, Solomon Schechter Schools, Atid, Nativ, KOACH, Conservative Yeshiva), NEXT (Birthright Israel Trips), Alumot (Livnot U'lehibanot), or FAN (B'nai Brith Youth Organization) and attend their next get-together. Your first boyfriend (Steve Fine from Camp Ramah the summer you turned thirteen) could turn out to be your last boyfriend (Steve Fine from the Camp Ramah reunion the summer you turned thirty). Nu, it was beshert.

You should also reconnect with old college friends. Well, not old college friends, obviously: you and anyone you went to college with are still young. At least according to the age you claim to be when someone asks. . . . Whether it's actually been a year or two or several since you've been on campus, get back in touch. Did you pledge AE Phi or SDT? Were you active in KOACH, Hillel, or JLIC? Join their alumni groups, get on their mailing lists, and get to their next happy hour. Yes, you should even attend your sorority's all-girl alumni tea. Those former sisters of yours all have brothers: nice Jewish brothers.

# SLUMBER PARTY

If you have a few free days, get away on a singles Shabbaton, a young adult con-
ference, or a weekend retreat. The United Jewish Communities (UJC), The
Jewish Federation, Limmud, Jewlicious, Elat Chayyim, and even your local synagogue, all sponsor conferences that are entertaining, educational, and, well,
jam-packed with Jewboys. And like a diner in a kosher deli, you know you can
have anything on the menu—every man there has a hechsher. So attend a few
panels, contribute to some discussions, and stay up all night chatting dorm-style
with fellow delegates. Or stay up all night doing something else dorm-style.

# YOU SCHTUPPED ME ALL NIGHT LONG

Speaking of dorm-style, you can't talk Jewish dating without discussing the oy
of sex. Let's say you meet a man at the Vodka Latke; how long should you wait
until you see his matzah balls? In the Torah the word for sex comes from the
root *Yod-Dalet-Ayin* meaning "to know." Just like keeping kosher elevates eating to a higher level, schtuping elevates your relationship to a higher place. For
that reason, Judaism upholds that sex is for married folks only. Observant Jews
adhere to this law; liberal ones not so much. They tend to schtup out of wedlock. Not that you know anyone like that. . . .

In general, Judaism teaches that sex is a good—no, a great—thing. It's not a
source of sin, it's a source of pleasure. It's not just for procreation, but also recre-
ation. That's one of the built-in bonuses of dating and marrying a nice Jewish
boy. Jewish husbands are commanded to provide their wives with three essential things: food, shelter, and a good schtup. Right up there with "Thou shall
not kill" is "Thou shall satisfy your wife." Ladies, Jewish women are not commanded to reciprocate. Traditionally Jewish men had privileges like wearing
tallit, counting in a minyan, and reading from the Torah. Meanwhile Jewish
women had the privilege of getting their candles lit on a regular basis. What
other religion gives you that kind of guarantee?

The Talmud even dictates how often a Jewish man is required to make his
wife happy. It's all based on his career. So when you're dating Jewish men
remember: if a man's a sailor he's commanded to satisfy his wife at least once

every six months; a camel driver—once a month; a donkey driver—once a week; a laborer—twice a week, and if a man's an independent contractor or has a private practice, he's commanded to satisfy his wife every single day. That explains why so many Jewish doctors and lawyers go into private practice—and why so many Jewish women want to marry them.

· · · · · · · · · · · · · · · · · · · · · · · · · · · · · · · · · · · · · · · · · · · · · · · · · · · · · · · · · · · · · · · · · ·

# TO JEW OR NOT TO JEW, THAT'S THE TOUGH QUESTION

Let's talk about marrying Jewish men. You're stuck between a rock and a heart place. Your current man is the smartest, funniest, friendliest, kindest, hottest guy you've ever met—but he's not a M.O.T. He might seem perfect, but he'd be even more perfect if he was part of the Jew kid club. Why? Shared culture, shared holidays, shared life. Manischewitz is thicker than water.

We've all heard the stats. According to the United Jewish Communities National Jewish Population Study:

- **47% of American Jews who got married in 1996 or after are married to a non-Jew.**
- **96% of children who have two Jewish parents are raised to be Jewish, compared to only 33% of children with intermarried parents.**
- **In all-Jew couples, 88% light Chanukah candles and 85% attend a Passover Seder; in intermarried couples 53% light candles and 41% attend a Seder.**

But like baseball stats, political polls, and my driver's license weight, numbers are just numbers. Not that the mixed marriage stats—or my driver's license weight—aren't alarming, but the decision to go Jew or go home is about more than just numbers. At least it was for me.

In high school I followed my folks' strict "only-date-Jews" rule, but in college, I fell for a Catholic kid. Clearly my parents were meshuggene, because it didn't matter at all that my guy was a goy boy; we had a fun, loving relationship. Well, we did until he said, "If we ever get married and have a baby boy, we should have the bris and the baptism in the same weekend, so our out-of-town guests could be here for both."

His idea was totally logical, totally fair, and had me totally *farmisht* (shook up). My brain started turning at spin-cycle velocity. A baptism? I could handle watching my baby boy get his penis chopped—that's no biggie—but baptized? Oy vey iz mir! My baby needs a baptism like he needs a loch in kop.

That was the moment I decided to only date within The Tribe. Not just because my parents told me to, but because my heart told me to. If I wanted to marry a Jewish boy, I should only date Jewish boys. And I realized right then and there that I wanted to say "I do" to another Jew. Yup, Moses had a burning bush, Noah had his big boat, Abe had that whole kill-your-son-just-kidding-thing, and this Jewish babe had a drunken 2 AM discussion about my make-believe baby boy's near baptism-bris double-feature. But that bap chat made me realize: I want a Jewish home, a Jewish life, and a Jewish husband. I really want a Jewish husband; seriously why is that taking so long? I want to marry someone who shares my connection to Torah and Israel, my love for seders and Shabbat, who know his bagels from his bialys, and his smoked fish from his lox. Plus, I like my guys circumcised. So for me, the J-factor is a dealbreaker. I want to stand under the chuppah with a man who always imagined getting married under one. Or at least would have if any Jewish man anywhere ever stopped to imagine his wedding day.

That being said, I know my choice is personal and isn't everyone's. There are plenty of Jew girls dating non-M.O.T.s and lots of shiksas dating Jew boys. I encourage all of you to bring a little Judaism into your relationship. Organizations like the Union for Reform Judaism, the United Synagogue of Conservative Judaism, and the Jewish Outreach Institute offer a large variety of resources for interfaith couples. Local synagogues of every affiliation have outreach committees that sponsor social events, educational initiatives, and cultural programs that help mixed couples feel like a part of the congregation. Welcome aboard, we're expecting you.

## C'MON IN, THE MIKVAH'S WARM

Then there's the big C. No, not the big J.C., the big C . . . Conversion. If you're considering conversion, the first step is finding a rabbi you relate to. Every movement and shul does things a little differently, but the conversion process often involves attending an Intro to Judaism class, conducting one-on-one study sessions with a rabbi, and incorporating Jewish rituals into your life. On the day of your conversion, you'll take a dip in the *mikvah* (ritual pool) and appear before a *Bet Din* (religious court of three Jewish adults). You're now an official Member of the Tribe. Mazel Tov! (As an official M.O.T, you can now throw around phrases like Mazel Tov with reckless abandon).

If your boyfriend is the one converting to Judaism, he has to do all of the above plus get circumcised. Ouch! Even if your goy boy's already been snipped, he still needs a *Hatafat Dam Brit*, a ritual bris that draws a pinpoint of blood. Talk about proving his love. To marry his nice Jewish girl, he's not just buying you an emerald-cut; he's getting his own schmekel cut. Is he your mensch? I think so.

# THE TEN COMMANDMENTS
# OF JEWISH DATING

1. I am your girlfriend who brought you out of the dating pool.

2. You shall have no other girlfriends but me.

3. You shall not use the wrong name in bed.

4. You shall remember date night and keep it unholy.

5. Introduce me to your mother and father. And all your friends.
   And call me your girlfriend.

6. You shall not murder my dream of a big wedding.
   A really big wedding.

7. You shall not commit adultery. Yes, booty-texting, -tweeting,
   and -calling count.

8. You shall not steal all the covers from me in the middle of the night.

9. You shall not lie about where you were last night.

10. You shall not covet, or even check out, your neighbor's hot girlfriend.

# CHAPTER 7

# FRIDAY NIGHT LIGHTS
## (SHABBAT)

And on the seventh day, God rested. Well, apparently God wasn't single. For us single girls, Shabbat's not a day of rest; it's a day of work. Or at least a day of working it.

Friday nights are supposed to be my chance to unwind, to go home and relax, to take off my flats and stay awhile. Believe me, I'd love to do that; but I can't. I'm never going to meet a cool guy sitting on my couch, drinking Manischewitz by myself. If I want to meet my mensch, I have to be proactive, I have to put myself out there, I have to go where the action is. Or at least go where I can get some action. And statistically speaking, Shabbat shindigs are where it's at.

If I head out to a random dive bar or a Sunset Strip club, my chances of meeting an exciting, inspiring guy are low. An exciting, inspiring, good-looking guy—very low. An exciting, inspiring, good-looking guy who's had a bris? Forget about it. But if I get my pupik to a Shabbat celebration, it's jam-packed with Jewboys. It's like shooting gefilte fish in a barrel. There's no way I leave without a Coach clutch full of digits, which is I why I make the seventh-day rounds.

On Fridays I do singles' services at shul or Shabbat dinners with friends. Then I pull a double-shift and swing by a Shabbat lunch on Saturday. And sometimes I work overtime and hit up a Havdalah after that. The whole thing's exhausting. I'm running all over town. I'm burning the Shabbat candle at both ends. But I have to. Shabbat is prime mensch-hunting time; and if you don't schmooze, you lose.

This Friday night I'm getting my Shabbat on at my friend Aaron's. Once a month he hosts a Shabbat dinner and discussion and always invites an engaging group of eligible guys. Professional, successful, charming: is there a doctor in the house? Let's hope so.

I arrive at Aaron's and am greeted by tough competition. And Aaron. He says hi. But one glance around his pad, and it's clear I'm not the only Shabbos-hopping hottie in the house. I see Lisa, the bubbly blond entertainment lawyer; Jen, the yoga-loving ad exec; and Michelle, the brand manager with the big fake mondlen. These Jewish girls will fight tooth and manicured nail to get their guy. But I'm not intimidated; they can't hold a Havdalah candle to my mad flirting skills.

I quickly scope out the scene for fresh kosher meat. Bingo—tall handsome Heeb in the living room. Jen's busy talking at him, but not for long. When dinner's ready, I casually force my way into the spot next to him. Turns out Jay's a CFO, coaches Little League ball, and is even cuter up close. I definitely wouldn't mind fiddling on the roof with him later. We chitchat through Kiddush, and by Hamotzi I have him eating out of my hands. Or at least eating the challah I passed him with my hands. I flirt through dinner and close the deal during dessert. Is it a restful Shabbat? No. An effective one? Yes. Jay and I are meeting for margaritas on Sunday.

Saturday afternoon I head to Shabbat lunch at Laura's. She runs with a different tribe, so I have a new crop of candidates to pick from. I'm not into the dot-com dude or the Ph.D. guy, but hello Mr. Commercial Real Estate. He's got a cocky smile, an MBA, and is wearing tuchus-friendly jeans. I know his type and decide to go with my signature Netilat Yadayim strategy. I slide behind him in line for the sink, make small talk while we wait, then gently brush my ringless fingers against his as he passes me the pitcher. That's when the sparks start flying. Or when they would start flying if it wasn't Shabbat and I could light sparks. Or set off fireworks. Or create some electricity. We spend most of lunch talking and the rest of lunch laughing. He asks about my writing, I ask about the market, he asks me out. Just goes to show, hard flirt is the key to success.

I know this wasn't what God had in mind when he first created Shabbat. But things were different during Week One: dating wasn't this much work. Poor little Adam thought it was bad to be alone and poof! God gave him Eve. Well, we're not in Eden anymore, Toto. Nobody's magically turning my rib into a date or even taking me out on a date for ribs. Men don't just spontaneously appear in my garden. God's not serving them up on a fig leaf. I have to go out and find them. There's no rest for the wicked—or the wickedly hot.

The word *Shabbat* comes from the root *Shin-Bet-Tav*, which means "to rest, to cease, or to end." As in, when will it all end? When can I stop working so hard to hook a husband? When will all this hard work finally pay off? I honestly don't know. I'm sure someday I'll meet the mensch of my dreams, and we'll be able to sit back, relax, and enjoy the Shabbos together. Until then I work hard for the honey.

# KICKIN' IT GOD STYLE

Shabbat is all about eating, drinking, dancing, and napping. It's like reliving your Alpha Epsilon Phi days. Minus the walk of shame. Unless you don't drive on Shabbat, then the walk of shame is within the realm of possibility. But don't worry, no one will think you're walking home from a Friday night nookie; they'll think you're walking toward a Saturday morning service. In the same kippah you wore yesterday.

## DAY SEVEN SPIEL

We've all heard the story: God created the world in six days and rested on the seventh. Wait. Why doesn't the story finish with Day 6? On the sixth day God finished creation—The End. Why even mention what God was doing on the seventh day? It's like saying Snow White and the Prince lived happily ever after—and the next day they went to the beach. What Snow did the next day is irrelevant. But what God did the next day was genius! God could have gotten a head start on his next miracle, practiced his plagues, or perfected his burning bush trick, but he didn't. God pulled a Bueller and took the day off. Creation moves pretty fast. If you don't stop and look around once in awhile, you could miss it.

To ensure that we followed his example, God gave us Commandment Number Four: Remember the Sabbath and keep it holy. Shabbat didn't make the top three, but it's the upper half. Not bad, considering it's the only holiday that gets any billing in The Big Ten. The Twin Tablets make no mention of Yom Kippur, Sukkot, or Chanukah. Why the special Shabbat shout-out? Those other holidays happen once a year. Shabbat pops up every week, and God says we should look forward to it every day. And who's going to argue with that?

## T.G.I.S. (THANK GOD IT'S SHABBAT)

You are. You don't want to give up your weekends to uphold an ancient tradition. Well, you don't have to. Ever come home from work on a Friday night exhausted? You open a bottle of Merlot, decide not to go out, and sink into your couch? That, my friend, is Shabbating. Ever go to a friend's place for dinner on Friday night? You down a few drinks, eat a good meal, and toast the end of a stressful week? That's also Shabbating. How about Saturday brunch with the girls? Saturday afternoon nap? Saturday afternoon delight? You just had a Shabbat. Three times.

Celebrating Shabbat doesn't ruin your weekend; Shabbat's the reason you have a weekend. It's the first personal day, the foundation for vacation, the original summer Friday. Today everybody's working for the weekend. But in ancient times, there was no weekend. Sure, the Kings and Pharaohs could take a break, but the blue-collared shepherds worked 24/7 until the word came down from way upper management: thou must take the day off.

## LABOR LAWS

Not only can't you clock in on Shabbat, but the Talmud outlaws thirty-nine categories of *melachot* (acts of creating). This list of illicit work includes slaughtering, demolishing, dyeing, tying, baking, cooking, writing, kneading, weaving, grinding, tearing, and sewing. And of course, lighting and extinguishing fire. The rabbis based this list on acts you'd perform while rebuilding the Temple. Which is something most women do every Saturday right between their mani-pedi and power yoga . . . Temple building. Since synagogue construction isn't at the top of every Jew's to-do list, folks follow these Sabbath laws to varying degrees:

- You can't carry *muktza* (tools used to work); so leave your money, calculators, and tool belt at home. But keep your Gucci belt on. It's cute. Where'd you get it?
- You can't think about work. Of course now that I said that, it's all you'll be able to think about. Stop. Now. Think happy thoughts. Think dirty thoughts. There you go. Clean slate. Blank mind. Great! So whatever you do, don't start thinking about work again. And . . . you just did.
- Generating electricity is the same thing as starting a fire. So Shabbat's turnoffs include computers, TVs, and hair dryers. Shabbat's turn-ons include candlelit dinners, watching the sunset, and long walks on the beach.
- If you're *shomer Shabbos* (Shabbat observant), driving is a no-go. Sure hope those Prada boots are made for walking.

• • • • • • • • • • • • • • • • • • • • • • • • • • • • • • • • • • • • • • • • • • • • • • • • • • • •

# LET'S GET THIS SABBATH STARTED

Resting is one part of Shabbat; celebrating is the other. And everything you need to host a fun, frugal Friday night can be found in your happening bachelorette pad. Ditch the white linen table cloth. Forget the silver candlesticks. And stop waiting until you have a family—or an invite. Now is the time to get your Shabbat on. Host a Shabbat dinner party. Throw a Havdalah happy hour. Sleep in . . . with someone. Shabbat is not about using the good plates. It's about celebrating the good times.

It doesn't matter if the last time you did the whole candle-Kiddush-challah deal was just after you won the crazy dance contest at your Bat Mitzvah. You still have the moves. If not, here's a quick cheat sheet:

## CANDLE LIGHTING

We've all lit up before. It can be very relaxing. The Shabbat candles should be lit eighteen minutes before sundown by the woman of the house. Or condo. Or in my case, studio apartment. Some women cover their eyes while reciting the blessing so they can't see the fire until the Sabbath starts. Some women love surprises. The rest of us Google our blind dates so there are no surprises.

Many women also circle the flame three times with their hands to *kabbalat Shabbat* (welcome the Sabbath). And to dry the last-minute nail polish they threw on as their guests arrived. I'd guess O.P.I.'s Day of Rest Red.

If you don't have silver candlesticks, don't worry. God did not command us to buy a box of Rokeach's white Shabbat candles and place them in our sterling sticks. Tea lights, votives, pillar candles, vanilla candles—they can all burn, baby, burn. Shabbat candles just need to be large enough to burn through dinner and small enough to burn themselves out. You can't blow the candles out; blowing is considered hard work. But I don't need to tell you that.

## KIDDUSH (SANCTIFICATION)

The rabbis understood that after a long week at work, nothing's more relaxing than a glass of red wine. Except a bottle of red wine. Or a magnum. So fruit of the vine it is. Technically, you can use grape juice instead of wine. You can also wear generic instead of designer. No one I'd hang with would do either.

To ensure a good pour, our old friends, the rabbis, declared that a Kiddush cup must contain at least 3.3 ounces of wine. But they didn't declare what kind of cup counts; so no fancy goblet required. Any chipped wineglass, Cathy mug, or souvenir tumbler from a ZBT party will do. Remember, it's not the size of the cup for the wine; it's the size of the wine in the cup.

After you fill your cup, recite the blessing over the wine, and take a big swig. All your guests are then required to partake of the wine as well. What? No one likes to drink alone.

## NETILAT YADAYIM (WASHING OF THE HANDS)

All employees must wash their hands before returning to not working. So armed with a two-handled pitcher, you pour water over your hands three times (right, left, right) and recite the blessing. Because you're purifying yourself before breaking bread, the hand-washing and challah-eating are considered one act. This means you can't talk between the two. You must be vewy, vewy quiet. We're hunting wabbits, or wabbis, or chatty yentas like me. Hmph. No comment. Not that I could comment because I can't talk. I won't say anything. Not a word. This is me not talking. All quiet on the Shabbat front.

## HAMOTZI

Now that you have light, booze, and clean hands, it's time to eat the only carb you'll let yourself near all week. The challah is the braided egg bread that we serve especially on Shabbat. In ancient times, eggs were often hard to come by. So daily bread was made without eggs, Shabbat bread with them.

The challah's three braided strands represent the commandment's three parts: to *Zachor* (remember) the Sabbath, to *Shamor* (keep it), and *B'Dibbur Echad* (do them as one act). It's also a mitzvah to make Shabbat a little fancier than the rest of the week. Like the French twist you wear to a wedding, the braid is the updo of breadstyles.

After the blessing, many Jews sprinkle salt on their challah. Why? To help support the kosher salt industry. Well, that and salt was used to accompany the offerings made at the Temple in Jerusalem. Today we have no Temple, so we make do with our table.

No need to freak out if you forget to pick up a challah. While it's tradition to use a challah on Shabbat, you can say Hamotzi over any unsliced bread—Kaiser roll, French bread, onion bagel, even a tortilla. Jews are equal-opportunity carbers.

## DOUBLE OR NOTHING

Some Jews are such big bread-heads, they serve *lechem mishneh* (double bread) on Shabbat. Why do we have two challahs on the table? While the Jews wandered the desert for forty years, God fed them manna from Heaven. Since God doesn't roll on the Sabbath, he'd deliver a double order of manna on Fridays.

## THE BIG COVER-UP

To continue the desert theme, the challah cover represents the dew that covered the manna. The cover also keeps the challah from getting jealous. You have the challah in third position behind the candles and wine. It's okay if you're seeing other rituals, but you don't have to do it right in front of the poor bread.

Now, nowhere does the Talmud say, "Thou shall use a silk challah cover your cousin Shlomo brought you back from Israel." So if you don't have a proper challah cover, go ahead and use anything you have lying around your apartment, like a tube top, a paper towel, or an Hermès scarf.

No matter how you cover it, a challah has one more important Shabbat function. Abundant experience has led me to a sacred, spiritual discovery: come Saturday morning, challah French toast is a miraculous hangover cure. Thank God.

# HAVDALAH

Shabbat officially ends when three stars appear in the Saturday night sky. At that point, you've done your duty, you've put in your Jewtime, and you can get back to work. Or not. Technically, there's one more thing you have to do. You can't just let your relationship with Shabbat fade out. You need to get closure.

*Havdalah* means separation or division. As in, we're separated, we're done, we're kaput. I know, I know, breaking up is hard to do. You don't know how you'll return to your old life; you're scared you'll never feel happy again. So our rabbis devised a way to get you out of your funk . . . the Havdalah happy hour. Invite your Heeb peeps over for a few Saturday night sunset cocktails and a little essen and fressen. Good food, good wine, and great friends, before you know it you'll be saying "Shabbat who?" Havdalah is the perfect preparty before the bars and the best way to say so long to Shabbat.

## WINE

To lessen the blow of the breakup, pour yourself a big glass of wine (and say the blessing over it). Don't drink it yet. It's for after you have The Talk, so you can drown your sorrows in Mogen David. Not only will the buzz take the edge off, but you'll be reminded that there are still a lot of sweet things in life. Like kosher wine.

It's recommended that you fill your wine cup until it's overflowing, so you have a week that overflows with good things. If you don't have any wine in the house, you can also use beer or liquor. Sometimes breakups call for the hard stuff.

## SPICES

There's Ginger Spice, Posh Spice, and now Havdalah spice. In a small container, tchotchke box, or bowl, combine cloves, allspice, nutmeg, cinnamon, and any other spice rack residents that you'd throw into a pumpkin pie. Now sniff. The soothing smell of the *b'samin* (spices) is supposed to calm your soul and mellow you out. As inhaling often does.

## HAVDALAH CANDLE

For Havdalah we light a special candle that has at least two wicks. Adam discovered fire on the first Saturday night, so we use multiple wicks to mimic his fire power. If you don't have a braided Havdalah candle hiding in your junk drawer, you can use any two candles you have in the house. Just hold them together so their wicks touch.

Once the candle is lit, many folks hold their nails up to the Havdalah flame. Some people say this scares off the bad omens for the week; others say your nails protect your fingers like Eden protected Adam. I say it's a chance to let everyone see that you're not sporting a ring.

Once you're lit up, gulp down most of the wine in the Kiddush cup, and then extinguish the candle in the rest. Since you don't completely burn down the Havdalah candle, feel free to reuse it next week. Reuse, recycle, and seriously, why should you have to drop another ten bills next Shabbat?

•••••••••••••••••••••••••••••••••••••••••••••••••••••••••••

# SHABBAT AND THE SINGLE GIRL

Now that we've got the Shabbat basics down, I want a word with the relaxed Almighty. Single women get their Shabbat on with the best of them, and yet we're getting the short end of the candlestick. We do all the work and get none of the perks. I love Shabbat as much as the next Jew, but I can't rest until something changes.

## LECHA DODI

Every Friday night, Jews sing Lecha Dodi, a traditional song that welcomes the Sabbath Bride. ("Lecha dodi likrat Kallah"—"Let's go, my friend, to greet the bride"). I don't understand; why does she have to be a bride? Why can't we welcome the Sabbath Babe? Why does it always have to be about the girl in the veil and the long white dress? The Sabbath Babe makes so much more sense! She can be lovely, beautiful, and *mekor haberachah* (a wellspring of blessings), but she's not talking marriage. She's cool with the way things are . . . for now.

## LET THERE BE LIGHTS

Don't get me started on the candles. We light two Shabbat candles for the two times the fourth commandment pops up in the old Torah (Exodus and Deuteronomy). But there are some rabbis who say single women should only light a single candle; you have to be married to light two. Makes perfect sense. Obviously if you're single, you'd never realize the fourth commandment appears twice in the Torah. That glaring detail can only be revealed with a secret diamond engagement decoder ring. . . . Ring or not, most modern girls light two candles.

## DOUBLE YOUR PLEASURE

Let's talk sex. A man is commanded to satisfy his wife on Shabbat. It doesn't say anything about a wife having to please her man. Which means, ladies, we can just savor the show. But don't get excited yet. It's a mitzvah to get down . . . with your husband. And a double mitzvah to do it on Shabbat . . . with your husband. That means a Jewish girl can have as many Shabbat schtups as she wants, but it doesn't count as a double bonus round unless she's married. So my extracurricular activities aren't earning me any extra credit. Tell me, Rabbi, why does a lot of sex with one Jewish man count for more than a little sex with a lot of Jewish men? How about a little thanks for single-handedly keeping so many Jewish men excited about dating Jewish women? Or a couple brownie points for hitting all twelve tribes?

## SINGLE WOMEN OF VALOR

And then, of course, there's *Eshet Chayil* (A Woman of Valor). Every Shabbat, Jewish husbands worldwide sing this King Solomon poem to their wives, giving weekly mad props to the married gals. "Her price is far above rubies . . . she's robed in strength and dignity, and cheerfully faces whatever may come." I'm sure their wives are strong and dignified and greet them with a cheery "Hi, Honey" when they walk through the door. But what am I, chopped liver? Nope. I'm chopped liver on fresh rye with a slice of onion, a dill pickle on the side, and a cherry phosphate to drink. And with New York deli prices, a meal like that will cost you a lot more than a ruby will. So don't tell me I'm not full of valor. And strong? I get my schvitz on in spin class. And happy? Don't I sound happy? But who's serenading the single gal? Who's giving kudos to the girls without ketubahs? Who's applauding the triumphant bachelorette? I am. That's who. And you should, too. Yes, you, in the Juicy sweatsuit. We single girls need to stick together. So next Friday, give a little Shabbat shout-out to one of these single women of valor:

- In 1950 our girl Gertrude Elion discovered a compound that led to a little something known as the first cure for leukemia. No biggie. Then this single woman of science discovered compounds that combated fatal viruses like hep, malaria, and AIDS. She got the Nobel Prize in 1998; she got married in—oh wait, never. Behind every great man there's a great Jewish woman. But behind many great women there's just a great tuchus.

- We all know about Watson and Crick and their famous double helix. But do you know about their famous double-cross? Watson didn't make his discovery until after he took a sneak peek at Rosalind Franklin's confidential research. Just like a man to sneak around behind a woman's back. Franklin was the real genius. This single lady of the lab is now credited with cracking the DNA mystery. Watson's just a man who got caught with his lab coat down.

- There she is, Miss America. That's Miss. Not Mrs. Miss. Single. Unattached. And, by the way, Jewish. In 1945, Bess Myerson became the first—and only—Jewish woman to win the coveted crown. And the swimsuit competition.

- Millions of American immigrants have been greeted by a strong, stunning single woman. Not a woman and her husband. And their three kids. Nope, the Statue of Liberty stands alone as the symbol of freedom and democracy. So it's only appropriate that Lady Liberty's welcome was written by single Jewish poet Emma Lazarus. "Give me your tired, your poor," but not your ring. Seriously, get up off your knees.

• In 1972 Sally Priesand became America's first ordained female rabbi. This bright pioneer led her own congregation and broke the glass *bimah* (sanctuary platform) for thousands of female rabbis. She never married. Who needs a chuppah and a husband, when you've got chutzpah?

• Eight-year-old Yael Arad tagged along to her older brother's Judo lessons. There were no other girls to fight, so she did what any proper woman would do—she took down the boys. But those boys shouldn't feel too bad about getting beat by a girl. That feisty taga-long went on to win Israel's first ever Olympic medal when she grabbed the silver in Judo in 1992. She didn't grab a husband until 1995. Put that in your pamphlet on great Jewish athletes.

# EASY-BAKE CHALLAH RECIPE

Okay, ladies, the savvy hostess just grabs a fresh challah from the kosher bakery, wraps it in foil, and heats it up in the oven for a few minutes before her guests arrive. It gives the challah that warm, homemade feel without that stressful, homemade hassle. But if you're feeling feisty and are up for the challenge, here's a simple challah recipe that will make you look like a total babe of a balabusta.

1 PACKAGE INSTANT ACTIVE DRY YEAST

2 TABLESPOONS SUGAR, DIVIDED

1 ¾ CUPS WARM WATER, DIVIDED

2 TEASPOONS SALT

¼ CUP OIL

2 EGGS, BEATEN

4 ½ CUPS BREAD FLOUR, DIVIDED

1 EGG YOLK

In a large bowl, throw together the yeast, 1 teaspoon of sugar, and ¼ cup warm water. Let stand about 10 minutes until yeast dissolves and gets foamy.

Add the salt, oil, eggs, 1 cup water, and 1 tablespoon plus 2 teaspoons sugar, and stir to combine.

In a separate bowl, measure 4 cups of flour by spooning it into the measuring cup (rather than scooping flour from the container). This helps make the challah light and airy. And no one likes a heavy challah. Or a heavy girl. . . .

(continued on next page)

Gradually add the 4 cups of flour (about ½ cup at a time) to the liquid mixture and stir to combine. It's important not to just dump it all in. That's the baking equivalent of skipping foreplay.

Remove dough from bowl; knead it on a well-floured surface with your well-manicured hands for 7 to 10 minutes until smooth and elastic. You can slowly add in up to ½ cup of flour if needed to make the dough less sticky.

Place dough in well-greased bowl, cover it with a clean towel, and store it in a warm place so it can rise. Grab your iPod and go work out for 1½ to 2 hours, or until dough doubles in bulk.

Punch down the dough; divide it into three sections, rolling each into an 11- to12-inch rope. On a floured surface, braid the ropes like your mom used to braid your hair—minus the scrunchie.

Place the braided bread on a greased cookie sheet. Cover it with a clean towel and place it in a warm place for 1½ to 2 hours to rise. Go get a facial while waiting.

Preheat the oven to 375°F.

Beat the remaining egg yolk with ¼ cup water, and brush the egg wash over the bread to give it that Pantene shine. If you want to accessorize, now's the time to sprinkle sesame or poppy seeds on top. Or dare to go bare. . . .

Bake for 45 to 50 minutes, or until the crust is golden.

Mazel Tov! Your skin looks great, your homemade challah is impressive, and you burned enough calories at the gym to actually eat a slice.

# CHAPTER 8

# HAPPY JEW YEAR
## (ROSH HASHANAH)

Ian and I met at a dive bar in August. I ordered a tall vodka soda; I got a tall handsome Jew. Six weeks later we were still going strong. So for the first time in a long time, I had a date for New Year's Eve. I had a reason to get all faputzed, I had an excuse to straighten my hair, I had someone to kiss when the clock struck Mincha. So nu, what's the problem? Ian wanted to ring in The Rosh at the It Shul, the L.A. congregation that was the place to see and be seen. Oh, and also to pray. . . .

"I heard it's impossible to get in," said Ian. "But that's why I'm dating you, Little Miss Macher. Can you get us on the list for the VIP section?"

The smart, confident Jewess that I am, I said we should just go to the low-key Jew joint I usually hit up. Well, at least that's what I said in my head. Aloud, I said, "Of course, I have connections; I'll get us in no problem."

No problem, my tuchus! I was in major tsouris. Those High Holiday seats sell out faster than U2 at the Rose Bowl, and they cost twice as much. Of course, in all fairness the Rosh Hashanah show goes on for twice as long. Lucky us.

Regardless, I had to nab those tickets somehow. But High Holidays are the most highly attended event of the year. Every single Jew shows their punim in shul. I heard the It Shul service was so packed last year, it was standing room only—even when the Ark was closed. Why the big turnout? Services are like the NBA, most people don't care about the regular season; but now that we're in the Jewish playoffs, and Yom Kippur's a single elimination event, suddenly everybody wants seats to the big game. And not just any seats; courtside seats.

Even if I could get us into the It Shul, general admission just wouldn't do. And you could forget about bimah-obstructed view. To show Ian I was a sexy single Jew with pull, I had to get good seats to the main sanctuary, first-shift service. Not the second shift, the family service, or the annex location that broadcasts the rabbi's sermon on a screen. Seriously, those overflow folks should just stay at home and stream the service online or watch the highlights on JewTube.

Two days, three messages, and four e-mails later, I finally got through to Edie, the It Shul office manager. "Sweetie, there's a system. The longer you belong, the larger donation you make, the better seats you get. If you want orchestra seats on the aisle by the time your unborn kid is a Bar Mitzvah, you better donate now. Also, there's a two-year waiting list for Tashlich; you want me to put you down?"

I was up shtick's creek without a paddle. I wanted Rosh Hashanah to be perfect, I wanted the holiday to bring us closer, I wanted to wow Ian with our first-class seats, but I couldn't even swing standby coach. I looked everywhere. I scanned Craigslist, I checked eBay, I tried Stub Hub, I even called a shomer Shabbos scalper; no one had anything for the sold-out show. There wasn't even a Hebrew HotTix that would release day-of rush seats. It was time to face reality; when it came to scoring Rosh Hashanah seats, I was a day late and a shekel short.

I should have expected this. There's always so much pressure to have the perfect New Year's Eve, and it never turns out to be the brilliant night you want it to be. Parking is impossible, places are packed, and prices are jacked up all over. Were other Jew events like this? Did people fight over front-row seats at Mount Sinai? Did everyone want to be ringside for David vs. Goliath? Or is it only on Rosh Hashanah that we're scrambling for choice sanctuary seating? I don't understand why Rosh Hashanah services have become such a scene. Rosh Hashanah is supposed to be about *tzedakah* (righteous giving), *tefillah* (prayer), and *teshuva* (repentance). Which is why I decided to do the righteous thing, tell Ian the truth, and pray that he didn't break up with me.

"Ian, we can go to Rosh Hashanah services, we can celebrate together, I just can't get us on the list at the IT shul."

"C, that's totally fine. I don't care where we sit, as long as I'm sitting next to you."

And right then, I knew it really would be a Happy New Year.

••••••••••••••••••••••••••••••••••••••••••••••••••••••••••••

# RINGING IN THE ROSH

Tonight we're gonna party like it's 5999. The first half of Judaism's High Holidays, *Rosh* (head) *Hashanah* (of the year) is the Jewish New Year. Just like good old December 31, the Rosh is a time for celebration and reflection. It's a time to get your groove and your guilt on. It's a time of new beginnings, new goals, and new beaus. So first thing up? Jew Year's Resolutions.

By the time the Rosh rolls around, you've already broken all the resolutions you made back in December. You never lost those last five pounds, you still work in that cubicle, and let's be honest: you're still schtuping your ex. Well, here's your second chance at a fresh start. RH is an opportunity to make things happen, to get unstuck, to switch up your life. Where do you want to be a year from now? Besides on your honeymoon. . . . This Jew year I want to:

- ♥ Lose five pounds, for real this time, I swear
- ♥ Throw a Shabbat dinner party
- ♥ Throw caution to the wind
- ♥ Throw my ex to the curb
- ♥ Bake a challah
- ♥ Eat only one piece of homemade challah, as it goes straight to my poulkes
- ♥ Give tzedakah
- ♥ Volunteer for a Jewish cause

♥ Hang up a mezuzah

♥ Hang up on a booty call

♥ Look for a new job

♥ Bag a new Jewish boy

♥ Always insist that he cover his scroll

........................................................................................

# NEW YEAR'S EVE PARTY

The New Year's party kicks off on Rosh Hashanah Eve. There's no ball drop, and you might not want to pull out your silver sequined minidress just yet, but *Erev Rosh Hashanah* (Rosh Hashanah Eve) can be one good time. The meal is amazing and the services are short. Well, relatively short. At least Academy Awards–tolerable. So if you and your friends are holiday orphans, throw a New Year's Eve dinner party at your pad.

## TONIGHT'S SPECIALS

You don't need to be a Top Chef to pull off an impressive RH dinner. You just need a few hours, a couple shortcuts, and a glass of wine to keep you calm. So send out the Evite, sound the virtual shofar, and let everyone know—it's on. But what's a Jew to serve?

**ROUND CHALLAH:** On all other occasions, we like our carbs braided. But on RH, we bake a challah in the round. Why the change-up? Some claim a frustrated Rosh hostess couldn't fit her long braided bread for twelve on her round serving platter. Some say the earth is round, and since it's the earth's birthday, the challah is round. Most go with the Tevye sunrise-sunset theory; Rosh Hashanah marks the end of one year and the start of another. The round challah reflects this circle of life. Please don't start singing *The Lion King*.

**TAPUCHIM U'DVASH (APPLES AND HONEY):** On Shabbat we throw salt on the challah to recall the destruction of the Temple. But on RH we ditch the salty tears and dip the challah in honey. Why? Salt can cause bloating just when you need to squeeze into that new Tahari pencil skirt you bought to wear to shul. Plus honey symbolizes our hope for a sweet new year. As for the apples, Jews customarily eat the harvest fruit on holidays, and The Rosh coincides with apple-picking. Toss it together and you've got Tapuchim U'dvash. If you're throwing an RH bash, update the tradition with an apple-and-honey tasting. Serve several apple varietals (Braeburn, Gala, Fuji, Golden Delicious) and all sorts of honey. Try apple blossom honey, organic raw honey, or honey in a squeezable plastic bear; go full-on Winnie-the-Pooh—except maybe wear pants. The tasting is a great conversation starter; more than a few guys will throw out the oh-so-original, "Can I call you honey?" That pickup line never works. But the honey-tasting does—guests love it.

**FORSHPEIZ (APPETIZER):** My wise mom always served her famous matzah ball soup and a little chopped liver before services and the rest of her *yontif* (holiday) meal after. That way my brothers and I didn't spend the entire service kvetching about being hungry. It's not a mandatory move, but it's a smart one. Everyone knows a full Jew is a happy Jew. Besides, who doesn't like a little foreplay? I mean forshpeiz. So invite your Heeb peeps over for a Rosh Hashanah happy hour. Dish out wine, challah, and traditional apps like chopped liver, gefilte fish, and herring. You can also go a little less bubbe and serve kosher frozen apps like mini-potato puffs and all-beef cocktail dogs. This preparty puts people in a celebratory mood, gets the Manischewitz flowing, and lets single guests check out the talent. After Erev Rosh Hashanah services everyone returns to your place for a night of flirting, fressing, and fun.

**MAIN COURSE:** For dinner serve up old-school Jewish grub: matzah ball soup, apple raisin kugel, carrot tzimmes, kasha varnishkes, kishke, and hopefully-not-dry brisket or apricot chicken. There's an easy-to-make matzah ball soup recipe at the end of the next chapter, so stay tuned. Don't touch that dial. Not that TVs have dials anymore.

**ON TAP**: It's customary to drink wine, but feel free to serve specialty cocktails on the side. Pop open champagne to toast the New Year, or continue the apples-and -honey motif by pouring appletinis, hard apple cider, and hot apple cider spiked with cinnamon, mulling spices, and rum.

**HONEY CAKE**: The fruitcake of the Jews, honey cake is an often-served, rarely enjoyed RH tradition. This is one holiday dish you should feel free to ditch. The cake's sweetness suggests the start of a sweet new year. The cake's dryness suggests it's a waste of calories. If you're going to cancel out all those hours of warrior pose and downward dog, do it with moist apple cake, scrumptious chocolate babka, or melt-in-your mouth homemade rugelach. These treats symbolize a sweet year and still taste great. Tastes great, more filling. Can I get an Amen?

·······································································

# ROSH HASHANAH SERVICES

Rosh Hashanah's not just about eating, it's also about praying. Do you zone out during services? Absentmindedly braid the fringe on your tallis? Start counting the number of pages left to go? Whether you're the Cliff Clavin of your synagogue or an only-on-holidays Jew, Rosh Hashanah services can be challenging. But if you can make it through a bad blind date, you can make it through RH day. Here's a little help:

## ONE OF THESE THINGS IS NOT LIKE THE OTHER

High Holiday services differ from standard Shabbat services in several ways. If you attend Shabbat services, you'll notice. If not, well, then just pretend you notice. On High Holidays we read from a different prayer book. We trade in the everyday siddur for the High Holiday Machzor. In addition to the usual service fare, this supersized book contains bonus material we only recite during the High Holidays. If only God believed that less was more. We also break out *nusach* (special melodies) just for the occasion. Same lyrics, different music. No need to download the Jew tunes; the Chazzan will lead you in these.

## SHOFAR, SO GOOD

Speaking of music, let's talk about the horn section. For many Jews, the shofar is the highlight of services. In ancient times this ram's horn was blown more frequently, but today we only haul it out around the High Holidays. The shofar blast reminds us of the binding of Isaac (which we read on RH) and God's last-minute ram substitution. It wakes up our consciences so we see our sins more clearly. And it wakes up any congregants who fall asleep midsermon. If a High Holiday falls on Shabbat, we're not allowed to blow any shofars. Sorry, boys, not tonight.

You don't need marching-band experience to blow the shofar; you just need to know four notes. Tekiah is a continuous sound, shevarim is three broken sounds, teruah is nine staccato notes, and *tekiah gedolah* (large tekiah) is a supersized tekiah sounded at the end of the set. Congregants often pull out their stopwatches to measure who has the longest tekiah gedolah. Get your mind out of the innuendo: these are the holiest days of the year.

## THE SERVICE SCHEDULE

Rosh Hashanah services can get confusing. You stand up, you sit down, you stand up again, you sit down again. And you could swear you've said this prayer twice. Like a passenger on Oceanic 815, you're totally lost. Well, help has arrived. RH services are actually made up of several smaller services: Ma'ariv, Shacharit, Musaf, Mincha, and Tashlich. Here's how they break down.

### Ma'ariv (evening)

This opening service is like most of the Jewish men I date—short. Starting at sundown on Erev Rosh Hashanah, it usually lasts about an hour. Featuring familiar prayers like the *Barchu* (a call to prayer) and the *Shema* (declaration of one God), Rosh Hashanah Ma'ariv is similar to the standard Ma'ariv except tonight we're singing a different tune . . . and a lot more of us showed up to sing it.

## Shacharit (morning)

It's New Year's Day and not a bowl game in sight, just a long day of prayer ahead of you. Shacharit starts as early as 8 AM, but lots of Jews sprint in around ten for the Torah reading. The first day Torah portion covers the birth of Isaac and the second day covers the binding of Isaac. The Shacharit service also features the *Amidah* (standing), which is the meat and potatoes of daily Jewish prayer. If you're Jew-ish, you may know the Amidah as the ten minutes you stand silently daydreaming until you see other congregants finish the prayer and sit down. Shacharit also includes one of High Holiday's greatest hits, *Avinu Malkenu* (our Father, our King). This prayer reflects how we're both God's children and God's subjects. She's my daughter, my sister, daughter, sister kind of thing.

Heads-up: Most rabbis like to squeeze their sermon in at the end of Shacharit. Don't say I didn't warn you. . . . If you're not in the mood for learning, head to the lobby for some flirting. There'll be plenty of other single Jews skipping class out there.

## Musaf (additional)

This additional midday service contains the hit single "U'netaneh Tokef." This prayer asks who will live, who will die, and how they'll go. Who by fire, who by water, who by strangling, who by stoning, who by earthquake, who by plague, who by sword, who by beast—it's a very uplifting little ditty. . . .

Musaf also contains the longest Amidah of the year. Lots of Jews duck out sometime during this marathon remix; they have meals to prepare, guests to welcome, or are just plain shul-ed out. Some of the folks who leave early from God's big bash are the same ones who arrived late. Different from other New Year's parties, ladies, you may want to think about making more than an appearance at this one.

## Mincha (afternoon)

We're praying for keeps today. In many congregations it's only the diehards left now. Yes, sticking it out into this overtime period can be difficult. But remember, no matter how bored you get, it could always be worse. You could be fasting.

### Tashlich (cast away)

Tashlich is the Jewish version of cleaning out your Marc Jacobs purse. Good old prophet Micah said, "You will cast all sins into the depths of the sea." So on the first afternoon of Rosh Hashanah, we walk to a moving body of water and let our sins ride the waves. We recite a few prayers, toss breadcrumbs in the water, and empty our pockets of lint. Not that many Jews have pocket lint. The Chosen People tend to choose dry cleaning. If the first day of Rosh Hashanah falls on Shabbat, don't double-book; just move Tashlich to the second day.

### Would the real Rosh Hashanah please stand up?

Did I just say second day? Yes. Come sundown, we do it all again. I'm sure this won't be the first time you go for a second round. Why the repeat? A new moon can appear on one of two days each month, so the ancient Temple priests announced the official new moon (and thus the official New Year) through a flaming relay. They lit a torch in Jerusalem, which told neighbors to light a torch, which told their neighbors that the New Year started.

After the destruction of the Temple, Jews scattered to suburbs around the globe, so we switched to the two-day tradition. That way Jews living outside Jerusalem could be confident that one of the two days they celebrated on was the real Rosh Hashanah. Today calendars, Blackberries, and Outlook have replaced moon-watching, so Reform Jews believe we're all in sync and observe one day of Rosh Hashanah. Out of tradition everyone else still goes on a forty-eight-hour bender.

••••••••••••••••••••••••••••••••••••••••••••••••••••••••••••

# I'VE GOT THE GOLDEN TICKET

Now that you're a maven on RH services, you just have to decide where to spend them. Finding a place to pray on High Holidays is like finding a nice Jewish boy—overwhelming, frustrating, and something your parents keep bugging you about. Don't belong to a synagogue? Don't know other Jews in town?

Don't worry. You can beat the holiday hassle with a few smart moves.

Synagogues across the country welcome guests on the High Holidays. They open their doors—but be prepared to open your Prada wallet. A nonmember ticket to a synagogue's full High Holiday lineup runs from $150 to $400. And there's no gift with purchase, ladies. The good news is it's often general admission. If there's no assigned seating, you can snag a seat next to a cute single professional who could also afford to pay the full-price fare.

## PRAY FOR LESS

If you can't buy the ticket for face value, there are plenty of ways to pray for less. Do you wait for the Macy's One-Day Sale? Go back to The Gap for a one-time price adjustment? Clip double coupons from the Sunday paper? Well, put those bargain-shopping skills to work and find some name-brand services at discount prices.

- **Can't pay retail? Then *handel* (bargain). Many congregations offer tickets at steep student discounts or on a sliding scale. So get off your tuchus, call the synagogue office manager, and plead your case.**

- **Looking for a Sugar *Abba* (daddy)? Some synagogues offer sponsorship programs where wealthy congregants act as benefactors and purchase High Holiday tickets on someone else's behalf.**

- **There's also a national "buy once, get one free policy" that's perfect if you just moved to a new city or are spending the High Holidays with your long-distance beau. If you're a dues-paying member of one synagogue (or if your parents still list you on their membership), you can attend High Holiday services at most other synagogues of the same affiliation (Reform, Conservative, Orthodox, Reconstructionist, and Sephardic) for no cost. The second synagogue just needs confirmation of your first payment, so hold on to your original receipt, or ask your hometown shul to send a proof-of-purchase letter.**

- Were you a member of USY? Did you spend a summer at Camp Ramah? Attend a Solomon Schechter school? If your parents forced, err . . . encouraged you to participate in any Conservative-movement youth programs, check out Project Reconnect. The United Synagogue of Conservative Judaism teamed up with congregations across North America and Israel to offer free High Holiday tickets to twenty- and thirty-somethings who were once involved in their youth groups. Guess all those lame USY bowling nights paid off after all.

- Can't find a synagogue willing to cut their price? No worries, there are affordable ways to observe the High Holidays and make your rent. Don't feel weird about hunting for bargain-basement bruchas: everybody's doing it. In fact, you may find younger crowds at alternative digs like college Hillels. On the High Holidays, these Centers for Jewish Students open their doors to the public. Their services range from a dozen people davening in an English 101 classroom to hundreds of Jews congregating in a large campus ballroom. Hillel services are often free to students, discounted for alumni, and available for a small fee to the community at large. Pray and hang with undergrad hotties. Yes!

## PAY TO PRAY?

Many folks don't understand why synagogues charge for High Holiday services in the first place. Why is a religious experience all about money? And so much money? If you're throwing down two hundy for seats, shouldn't they be courtside at a Lakers Game, not Bimah-side at Beth Am? Here's the spiel:

Jews aren't supposed to carry money on Shabbat, so unlike other religions, we don't pass around a weekly collection plate. Instead, we collect money on the Big Days to keep the synagogue running year-round. Proceeds at the door benefit building funds, staff salaries, programming, books, and more. Yes, $150 to $400 may seem steep. But for the price of a cup of coffee a day you can keep the synagogue open all year. You can even enjoy the synagogue all year. To lure you back, most congregations let you put the cost of your High Holiday tickets toward their young adult membership fees. So you can get more for your money. Y'all come back now, ya' hear?

Not looking to join a shul? You're not alone. Lots of Jews belong to the only-on-High-Holidays club. Attendance soars during these days; so many synagogues hold services at large outside venues (hotel ballrooms, school auditoriums, theaters). The cover charge helps pay for the rented space, tables, and chairs. Congregations also hire private security at these services. The physical tickets help keep track of who enters the building, and ticket prices help pay for Bruno at the door.

The good news is, no matter how much you spend on the High Holidays, it's all tax-deductible. Tickets purchased from synagogues, Hillels, and other nonprofits can go on your tax forms in April. Even Uncle Sam wishes you *L'shana Tovah* (Happy New Year).

# THE JEWISH "CHALLAH" DAYS CRIB SHEET

Rosh Hashanah kicks off a Hebrew calendar that's packed with holidays. Since these celebrations are based on a lunar calendar, their dates in the secular calendar are always moving around. Of course knowing how flaky Jewish guys can be, you're probably used to having your dates rescheduled by now.

And remember, holidays all start at sundown—Jews don't like to wait until midnight to get the good times going.

## HOLIDAY: ROSH HASHANAH

**WHAT IT IS**: Jewish New Year
**WHEN IT IS**: 1–2 Tishrei (September)
**WHAT WE EAT**: Apples and Honey
**WHAT WE DO**: Ring in the New Year

## HOLIDAY: YOM KIPPUR

**WHAT IT IS**: Day of Atonement
**WHEN IT IS**: 10 Tishrei (September/October)
**WHAT WE EAT**: Nothing
**WHAT WE DO**: Live life in the fast lane

## HOLIDAY: SUKKOT

**WHAT IT IS**: Fall harvest festival
**WHEN IT IS**: 15–21 Tishrei (October)
**WHAT WE EAT**: All our meals al fresco
**WHAT WE DO**: Shack up

## HOLIDAY: SHEMINI ATZERET

**WHAT IT IS**: Eighth day of Assembly

**WHEN IT IS**: 22 Tishrei (October)

**WHAT WE EAT**: Sukkot leftovers

**WHAT WE DO**: Pray for rain

## HOLIDAY: SIMCHAT TORAH

**WHAT IT IS**: Rejoicing with the Torah

**WHEN IT IS**: 23 Tishrei (October)

**WHAT WE EAT**: Celebratory sweets and signature cocktails

**WHAT WE DO**: Some finish what they start: Jews start what we finished

## HOLIDAY: CHANUKAH

**WHAT IT IS**: The Festival of Lights

**WHEN IT IS**: 25 Kislev–1 Tevet (December)

**WHAT WE EAT**: Latkes and sufganiyot

**WHAT WE DO**: Small triumphs over large—men everywhere rejoice

## HOLIDAY: TU B'SHEVAT

**WHAT IT IS**: New Year of Trees

**WHEN IT IS**: 15 Shevat (February)

**WHAT WE EAT**: Four courses of wine and fruits

**WHAT WE DO**: Give a hoot, don't pollute

## HOLIDAY: PURIM

**WHAT IT IS**: The Story of Esther

**WHEN IT IS**: 14 Adar (March)

**WHAT WE EAT**: Hamataschen and lots of alcohol

**WHAT WE DO**: Play dress–up

## HOLIDAY: PASSOVER

**WHAT IT IS**: When WE came forth out of Egypt

**WHEN IT IS**: 15–22 Nisan (April)

**WHAT WE EAT**: Matzah

**WHAT WE DO**: Seder it up

## HOLIDAY: YOM HASHOAH

**WHAT IT IS**: Holocaust Remembrance Day

**WHEN IT IS**: 27 Nissah (April)

**WHAT WE EAT**: A meal with the mishpacha

**WHAT WE DO**: Never forget

## HOLIDAY: YOM HAZIKARON

**WHAT IT IS**: Israel Memorial Day

**WHEN IT IS**: 4 Iyar (April/May)

**WHAT WE EAT**: Israeli food

**WHAT WE DO**: Honor Israeli soldiers

## HOLIDAY: YOM HA'ATZMAUT

**WHAT IT IS**: Israel Independence Day

**WHEN IT IS**: 5 Iyar (April/May)

**WHAT WE EAT**: Hummus, kabobs, falafel, and pita

**WHAT WE DO**: Tonight we're going to party like it's 1948

## HOLIDAY: LAG B'OMER

**WHAT IT IS**: 33rd day of counting the omer

**WHEN IT IS**: 18 Iyar (May)

**WHAT WE EAT**: Barbeque

**WHAT WE DO**: Have fun in the sun

# HOLIDAY: SHAVUOT

**WHAT IT IS**: Receiving the Torah
**WHEN IT IS**: 6–7 Sivan (May/June)
**WHAT WE EAT**: Only dairy
**WHAT WE DO**: Pull an all-nighter

# HOLIDAY: TISHA B'AV

**WHAT IT IS**: Falling of the temple
**WHEN IT IS**: 9 Av (July)
**WHAT WE EAT**: Nothing
**WHAT WE DO**: Sit on the ground during prayer

# HOLIDAY: SHABBAT

**WHAT IT IS**: Day of rest
**WHEN IT IS**: Every week, sundown on Friday–sundown on Saturday
**WHAT WE EAT**: Challah
**WHAT WE DO**: Nap. Schtup.

# CHAPTER 9

# NAUGHTY JEWISH SHUL GIRL
## (YOM KIPPUR)

I've been a bad, bad girl. And I stand before you on Yom Kippur to atone for my sins . . . and to advertise them. I want to get the word out. I want to sound the shofar. I want to let everyone know that Jewish girls can be bad, too. Think I've missed the point of Yom Kippur? Think I've lost my mandlen? Then you haven't hit the singles' scene lately.

Let's go live to a bar on Saturday night. I'm in the middle of flirting with this fine guy Nate when his dreykop buddy Dave says, "Nate, check out that hot blonde at the end of the bar."

As I turn to size up my competition, he adds, "She's rocking a Catholic schoolgirl skirt."

I hate her before I see her. Dave just interrupted my regularly scheduled flirt to point out another chick. And not just any chick—a naughty Catholic schoolgirl. Those plaid-skirted, knee-socked shiksas are always pulling the barstool out from under me. It's not fair. I want to be the object of men's desires. I want to be the stuff of men's dreams. I want to inspire the Halloween costumes of long-legged sorority girls everywhere. But how many men are fantasizing about the naughty Jewish schoolgirl?

None, but they should be. You don't have to be Catholic to be bad. My black patent-leather shoes shine up . . . and down and even upside down. Sure, Jewish day school uniforms don't exactly scream "come hither." But those long-sleeve shirts and floor-length skirts are just our way of playing hard to get. Or at least hard to get to. Underneath all those layers of clothing, we're easy like Shabbos morning.

In fact, we come from a long line of wild women. Eve started it all by eating an apple, and we haven't looked back since. Know how Ruth bagged Boaz? She snuck into his room in the middle of the night and satisfied his foot fetish. Know how Esther saved Shushan? She got all faputzed, got the king drunk, and touched his golden scepter. Know how Judith saved her town? She seduced a general, got him drunk, then cut off his keppe. Okay, so maybe that's more like crazy Jewish schoolgirl but close enough. And still no one knows that Jewish girls are in the naughty corner.

That's where Yom Kippur comes into play. Yom Kippur is our day to confess—no, brag—about our one-night stands. It's our chance to stand up and say I've been a naughty girl. And then sit down when the Ark is closed. And then stand up again when it opens. Yom Kippur is our opportunity to let God, the whole congregation, and the handsome man in the Armani suit sitting next to us know that we've committed a whole Viddui of sins this year. And we're so proud, we're pounding our chests about it:

We ACT perverse. We BLOW your shofar. We CHECK out your tuchus. We DANCE the horizontal hora. We ENJOY it. We FLIRT in shul. We GO meshuggene in bed. We HAVE fun. We INVITE you up. We JDATE and tell. We KISS and Facebook. We LET you dip your apples in our honey. We MOUNT your Sinai. We NOTICE your long yad. We OPEN a second bottle. We PLAY spin the dreidel. We can't be QUIET during services. We ROCK at kissing. We STOP, drop, and roll. Twice. We're UP for doing the double mitzvah. We VERIFY your bris. We WAKE your neighbors. We play eX games. We YANK the kosher salami. We're ZEALOUS in bed.

Ladies, we've got a long line of sins. We just need to sound the shofar, get the word out, and let men like Saturday Night Nate know: it's not either-or. It's not black or white. It's not milk or meat. They can marry a Jewish girl and misbehave with her, too.

So this Yom Kippur, help our cause. Don't say you're sorry, say you're sexy. Don't show remorse, show some poulke. Don't make amends, make a statement. You want the Jew? You can't handle the Jew.

As for Nate, I'm not one to get intimidated by a little shiksa competition. You think I'm going to let that Catholic girl nab my man? Over my hot body. I just bought a round of Patrón shots, brought my A-flirt, and let Nate know that I'm a naughty Jewish shul girl and I'm good times.

· · · · · · · · · · · · · · · · · · · · · · · · · · · · · · · · · · · · · · · · ·

# SAY YOU'RE SORRY

Okay, maybe *Yom Kippur* (Day of Atonement) shouldn't just be about earning a good rep for being bad. Sure, YK's the perfect day to show off our sins, but it's also the day we atone for them. So you should probably spend some time doing the apology thing. As the High Holiday's final act, Yom Kippur is the downer to the Rosh's upper, the hangover after the New Year's party. And like January 1, you'll spend Yom Kippur Day swearing you're never drinking, smoking, or sinning again.

· · · · · · · · · · · · · · · · · · · · · · · · · · · · · · · · · · · · · · · · ·

# YAMIM NORAIM

If Yom Kippur's the big game, then think of the *Yamim Noraim* (Days of Awe) as boot camp. Jews spend these ten days (sandwiched between Rosh Hashanah and Yom Kippur) getting their lives in shape. We think about the sins we've committed, the changes we should make, and the apologies we should issue. This is the time to make good.

What's with the YK warm-up? God's making his list and checking it twice.

On Rosh Hashanah, God starts writing names in the Book of Life. On Yom Kippur, he seals the book—with or without your name inscribed. So we spend the Days of Awe trying to get our name on the list at the door. The Who Shall Live Club is one you don't want to be denied entry from, and God is one bouncer who means business.

For many Jews the Days of Awe are like the Cannonball Run of remorse. They scramble all around town trying to sit down with family, meet up with friends, and make things right. And that's just the tip of the schmekel. Owe a big mea culpa? Send flowers. Owe a long-distance apology? Send a Jewish New Year's card. Owe an apology to everyone? Update you status. Jewgirl3 is "sorry for everything she's done to everyone she knows. Also, I'm in line at The Coffee Bean."

Why all the running around? If you sinned against God, then you apologize directly to the Big Guy. "God, I'm sorry I used your name in vain when friggin' Windows crashed again, and I'm sorry this is my first time at services in six months. Okay, fine, my first time at services in a year. So now I'm also sorry about lying in synagogue about the last time I was in synagogue."

But if you sinned against another person, a simple confession to the Chief isn't enough. First, you have to make things right with the person you wronged. She has to forgive you before God can clear you. That makes sense. It's not like you borrowed God's new dress without checking or drank the Almighty's last Amstel Light without asking.

## ARE YOU A GOOD WITCH OR A BAD WITCH?

My guess is a little bit of both. I bet you have a few sins up your three-quarter-length sleeves. And a few more up your hip-clutching jeans. And few stuffed in your bra. Have you ever snagged a maraschino cherry behind the bartender's back? Thou shall not steal. Have you ever faked a doctor's appointment because 2:00 Wednesday was the only time your salon could squeeze you in? Thou shall not lie. Have you ever let the saleslady give you twenty-five percent off a dress that wasn't on the sale rack? Thou shall not abuse the Nordstrom Half-Yearly Sale. Starting to feel guilty? We're just getting started.

Let's talk about your dating sins. Technically, you're not supposed to part your sea until you're married. Remember the law student you met in Miami? The architect from the wedding? The tour guide in Israel? That's a sin, another sin, and another well-worth-it sin. Look, I get it, men like their women like they like their martinis—*schmutzidik* (dirty). And believe me, I can be a dirty girl; I can talk dirty, I can act dirty . . . I don't even shower on Yom Kippur. But all that girls-behaving-badly stuff means I have some splainin' to do. And so do you—not just for the sins you committed with Jewish boys, but for the sins you committed against them.

Remember, Todd? He wasn't the hottest kreplach in the bowl, but you could have hit Reply. And Josh? You could have been upfront about seeing other people. And Sean? So he has a little dreidel; he still deserved a call back. You need to make amends. You need to make things right. So on your mark, get set, apologize.

## BETTER SAFE THAN SORRY

Atonement is a two-way street. It's not enough just to say "I'm sorry"; you also have to say "I forgive you." Part of this High Holiday clean-start program is letting go of your grudges. If you want people to accept your apology, you have to accept theirs.

Why are we forced to forgive? On the tenth day of Tishri (also known as Yom Kippur), Moses schlepped down Mount Sinai lugging the second set of The Ten Commandments. He told the Israelites that God forgave them for the whole golden calf disaster that led to the destruction of the first set of ten. If God can overlook a gigantic 14-karat bovine, you can forgive your friend for dating the now-bald dude you dated during college. And you can forgive your ex for schtuping that fake-blond girl who's still in college. Before you protest, remember God knows what he's doing. Just look jaw-droppingly hot when your ex drops by to apologize. You answer the door looking like a total babe—and you forgive him—he'll never forgive himself for letting you go. It's a win-win. You get into the Book of Life, and he spends his life pining for you. That God guy sure is smart.

# LIFE IN THE FAST LANE

Mazel Tov! You made it through Yamin Noraim, which means you're ready for Yom Kippur. If you were a contestant on *$100,000 Pyramid*, and Betty White said "Yom Kippur," you'd shout "Fasting." Because the number-one thing people associate with YK is the embargo on eating. From sundown on YK Eve to sunset on YK day, there's no essen, no fressen, no noshing. Why do we fast? Is God grounding us from the kitchen because we've been naughty little girls? Fasting helps us focus on the spiritual rather than the physical. It helps us think about the changes we want to make in our life and the kind of person we want to be this year. For me, not eating reminds me that this year, I want to be thin.

Fasting also resolves a time-management issue. Jews need to use every second of every minute of Yom Kippur to show our compunction. Our time to repent is running out. We can't take a break from our apologies to eat a meal. Even drive-thru fast food isn't fast enough. It's all atoning all the time.

With fasting, we also prove to ourselves that we can control our behavior. If we can resist eating, then we can resist any kind of sinning. If I can say no to a hot lunch today, then I can say no to a hot guy next week ... although I'd probably say yes to the hot guy next week and just atone for him next Yom Kippur.

## GET-OUT-OF-FASTING-FREE CARD

A few people don't have to fast. If you're pre-Bar/Bat Mitzvah age, elderly, sick, pregnant, or nursing, you're allowed to eat. So if you have a challah in the oven, you're in the clear. If you're feeding a little one, you're good to go. Surprise, surprise, the married girl with the baby is at the all-you-can-eat buffet while the single girl's on a diet. Well, that's just icing on the cake. Maybe checkerboard cake, or banana cake, or babka cake, or—why did I mention food?

## DON'T DRINK THE WATER

For observant Jews the twenty-five-hour fast covers more than just food. To practice complete self-denial, we're also supposed to abstain from wearing leather shoes, applying lotions, taking showers, and having sex. Not that anyone would want to have sex with someone who hasn't showered. The YK fast also includes all beverages, so there's no drinking and davening. There are no nonfat lattes, no low-carb protein shakes, and no overpriced bottles of water. To avoid getting parched while praying, most Jews eat a mild prefast meal on *Erev Yom Kippur* (YK Eve). You're usually looking at matzah ball soup (see recipe), baked chicken, boiled potatoes, steamed veggies, and challah. Yes, you'll be eating culinary beige, but you should eat a lot and eat early. Remember sundown means forks down. Once you've finished your last supper, you'll head to shul for services.

# YOM KIPPUR SERVICES

Your new boyfriend asked you to join him at Yom Kippur services. You can dress to impress, but bless to impress? Oy! You're happy to apologize. You're down with a zero-calorie day. But when it comes to YK services, you usually just stand when people stand, sit when people sit, and say Amen with the best of them. Don't worry—it's not a sin to feel confused. It's just a sin to let him know you do.

## DAY OF ATONEMENT ATTIRE

What should you wear for your Yom Kippur date? In some synagogues YK is synonymous with a fashion show. Jews dress their best in reverence to the importance of the holiday; and because they think a new outfit symbolizes the new person they want to become this year. Obviously nothing says "I've got my moral priorities straight now" like a new Calvin Klein suit.

In other shuls congregants wear all white. Like the white wedding dress you hope to be wearing soon, the white YK wardrobe represents moral purity. Reminiscent of the plain white kittel that Jews are buried in, it also reminds us not to take life for granted. Plus, it's an excuse to wear that cute white J. Crew sundress one more time after Labor Day.

Yom Kippur is also all about accessorizing. Typically, Jews only wear a tallis during morning services, but on YK we switch it up. We wear it in the evening (to Kol Nidre) and to every service on Yom Kippur Day. And there are a lot of them....

# SERVICE SCHEDULE

Like the Energizer Bunny, Yom Kippur services keep going and going and going. Similar to Rosh Hashanah services, they're actually made up of several smaller services: Kol Nidre, Shacharit, Musaf, Mincha, Ne'ilah, and Yizkor. Thinking of services in these smaller pieces should make them more digestible. Not that you should be digesting anything on a fast day.

## Kol Nidre (all vows)

This opening service begins at sundown on Erev Yom Kippur. It welcomes back any wayward Jews who strayed from following Jewish law, observing Jewish holidays, or stepping foot in a shul this year. Not that you know anyone like that. . . . A spiritual insurance plan of sorts, Kol Nidre also nullifies in advance any vows and promises we might break in the next year. I apologize now for anything I might screw up later. Not that I know I'm going to take part in any naughtiness next year, but I hope to. . . .

## Shacharit (morning)

Yom Kippur Day kicks off with Shacharit. This morning service contains the Torah and Haftorah reading. The Haftorah portion highlights Isaiah's famous sermon on fasting out of purpose, not obligation. You need to fast with meaning and passion. Unlike most men, God knows when you're faking.

The Shacharit service also features classic hits like the Viddui, the Amidah, and Avinu Malkeinu. While it's not necessary to know the entire Yom Kippur playlist, you should be familiar with the *Viddui* (confessional). This plea is made up of two prayers, Ashamnu and El Chet, both are alphabetical listings of sins we all commit. Many congregants tap their chest while reciting this confessional, to draw attention to their perky C cups. Well, that and to emphasize that the confession comes from their hearts. The "Stairway to Heaven" of Yom

Kippur, Viddui gets a ton of airplay. It's sung during every single YK service, so you'll hear it again and again and again.

## Yizkor (memorial)

Usually slotted between Shacharit and Musaf, this memorial service allows congregants to ask for forgiveness on behalf of the deceased and give charity in their honor. Giving tzedakah is said to lift the deceased's soul, and, let's face it, it's a chance for Jews to score extra points with God on Judgment Day. And we'll take all the help we can get.

Congregants also honor deceased loved ones by listing their names in the shul's Yizkor memorial book. You may know this book as the leaflet you flip through when you're bored during services or the pamphlet you fan yourself with when the AC is out. Yes, the sanctuary AC malfunction is a worldwide Yom Kippur phenomenon. It's not just a day of fasting; it's also a day of schvitzing.

Many Jews believe only people mourning a parent, sibling, spouse, or child should stay for Yizkor; it's bad luck for anyone else to participate. Hoping to avoid bad luck (and an extra thirty minutes of services), most young Jews head to the lobby during Yizkor. This makes it a prime-time to meet other single shul-goers.

## Musaf (additional)

Yes, some people duck out during this midday service. But if you stay, you'll be treated to the Avodah, a reenactment of the High Priest's YK service at the Temple in Jerusalem. But that's not all. We'll also throw in a long list of Jewish martyrs and the atrocities suffered by Jews all the way through the Holocaust. No, the fact that you have to fast for one single day is not considered an atrocity. In fact, it's a bonus. Your stomach looks amazingly flat in that new Yom Kippur dress.

## Mincha (afternoon)

This afternoon service means you're in the home stretch. Mincha stars our friend Jonah. This tale of forgiveness demonstrates God's desire to give man the benefit of the doubt and man's ability to live inside a one-bedroom fish. Bet your studio walk-up is sounding spacious right about now.

### Ne'ilah (locked)

Ne'ilah is like last call; it's your final chance to ask God to grant you another round. The ark stays open for the entire service and we stay standing for the entire time. At the end of Ne'ilah, the shofar is blown and Yom Kippur is officially over. Everyone makes a mad dash to the synagogue lobby to break fast with pareve shul brownies that taste deceivingly delish on an empty stomach.

# BREAK FAST FEAST

Post Ne'ilah, Jews gather in their homes to break the fast with family, friends, and fifty-five dozen bagels. And forty pounds of lox. And thirty tubs of cream cheese. YK's not a holiday without eating; it's a holiday between eating. It's atoning between meals, it's forgiveness between fressing. It's a day of apology sandwiched between a giant pre-fast meal and an even larger break fast one. The enormous break fast meal more than makes up for a day of dieting. You think it's a coincidence that we read the story of Jonah on Yom Kippur? It's God's way of warning us; if you bulldoze your way through break fast, you too will become a whale.

The break fast feast is traditionally dairy because it's easy to digest after fasting, the light color continues Yom Kippur's theme of purity, and, um, to be honest, I'm so hungry right now I can't remember the third reason.

This milchig meal is usually made up of bagels, bialys, cream cheese, tomatoes, onions, lox, smoked fish, blintzes, cottage cheese, kugel, and dessert. If you're hosting the meal at your house, try to organize a pre-service potluck drop-off. Ask your friends to come by with their dishes before services start, so you can all begin your break fast binge the minute services end. If your friends aren't down with potluck, don't get your tzitzit in a knot. It doesn't mean you'll get stuck cooking in the kitchen on a day when you can't eat. Many Jewish delis and restaurants sell carry-out break fast trays, so instead of making dinner, make a phone call and reserve one.

## SATISFY THEIR CRAVING

Whether you're hosting break fast or heading to a friend's, be prepared to flirt. Break fast parties are the perfect time to meet a man. Yom Kippur is a booty-free holiday, so men have abstained from food and fondling for twenty-five hours—and now they're craving both. Know how all the food at the grocery store looks tempting when you shop on an empty stomach? Well, all the girls at a party look tempting when guys flirt on an empty stomach. Forget about a match made in heaven, this is a match made in hunger. To those starving boys, every girl looks good enough to eat; and you need to make the most of their moment of vulnerability. See a boychik you like? Hand him his first plate of post-fast food, and he'll look at you in a whole new way. If you're the kind of girl who cares enough to bring him some creamed herring, then you're the kind of girl he could care about for life. Believe me, many a Jewish girl has met her beshert over break fast and bagels. So go get busy.

# NOT YOUR BUBBE'S MATZAH BALLS

What kind of modern balabusta has time to potchkeh with chicken bones and skim away schmaltz? Instead, just add water … and a few other things. Turn instant soup into an instant success by accessorizing with an array of vegetables. The veggies not only make the soup taste homemade, they make it look homemade. And let's be honest, ladies, appearances are everything. I promise you, no one will know the difference. Like your knock-off Prada purse, this semi-homemade soup looks just like the real thing.

2 PARSNIPS

3 STALKS CELERY

1 SMALL TURNIP

1 CUP PEELED BABY CARROTS

2 TABLESPOONS VEGETABLE OIL

2 EGGS

1 BOX SERVES 4 INSTANT KOSHER MATZAH BALL AND SOUP MIX
   (I USUALLY USE MANISHEWITZ)

You could cook your own stock . . . you could also color your own hair, but no trendy yenta does either.

Peel parsnips and cut into 2-inch pieces. Parsnips are my secret ingredient . . . which I just shared with every Jew out there.

Slice celery into 2-inch pieces.

Peel turnips and cut into small chunks. Stop kvetching. Yes, it's a pain in the tuchus to peel and cut the veggies, but it could always be worse. If you started from scratch, you'd be knee-deep in chicken necks and fleigels right now.

Add parsnips, celery, turnips, carrots, and soup mix package to 2½ quarts water, stir, and bring to a boil for about 30 minutes. Lower heat and allow to simmer for another 20 minutes, or until veggies are soft. Warning: the box contains two packets, the matzah ball mix and the soup mix. If you add the matzah ball mix to the boiling water, your soup will taste chaloshes (which is nothing like delicious).

As soup is cooking, get started on the matzah balls.

These matzah balls are so good, there's no need to admit they began life in a box. I know Yom Kippur's not the best time to stretch the truth, but what's one more bubbe maiseh. . . .

In a small bowl blend the vegetable oil and eggs.

Add matzah ball mix and stir. Be sure you don't use the soup packet in this step, or you'll have all kinds of tsouris.

Place the bowl in the refrigerator for at least 15 minutes.

This is where I part ways with the directions on the box. The box says to boil your matzah balls in the soup. Don't—your balls will sponge up all your broth and you'll be looking at a major soup shortage. Oy! Instead, in a separate soup pot, bring 2 quarts of water to a boil.

Once water is boiling, remove your matzah ball mix from the refrigerator. Wet hands and shape batter into balls about one inch in diameter. Don't pretend you don't know how large they normally are.

Drop the balls into the boiling water, cover the pot tightly, and let them simmer for about 20 minutes. Don't lift the cover: the trick to light and fluffy balls is to keep a lid on them. Hey, I said no peeking. . . .

Remove the matzah balls from the pot with a slotted spoon and add them to the soup pot.

If serving soon, simply let the combined soup and matzah balls simmer on low. If serving later, wait until combined soup and matzah balls have cooled, then store covered in the fridge. Reheat soup on stove top at low temperature.

**TIPS:**

• Reheating the soup actually intensifies the flavor, so make this the day before and reheat it on the day of.

• Feel free to slice, dice, or shape the vegetable pieces to your liking.

• You can also start with cans or cartons of kosher chicken broth and just add the veggies and matzah balls. (Soup and matzah ball mix are also sold separately).

# CHAPTER 10

# THE FESTIVAL OF LIGHTS. AND PRESENTS.
## (CHANUKAH)

Every December, Jewish girls everywhere do the Chanukah hustle, hoping to find a clutch gift for their great guy. We dodge in and out of stores, deciding, buying, regretting, and returning. It's a lot of pressure, time, and stress. A Chanukah present is a real relationship make-or-break. It's your chance to show your main man just how well you know him. Or reveal just how well you don't. Finding the perfect gift is harder than finding the perfect man. And we all know how hard that can be.

Who can retell the dates that befell us, who can count them? I can. Three new dates a month times twelve months a year times sixteen years of dating. Minus the time off for good relationships. Plus the random hookups, the one time I was stood up, and the guy whose name I can't remember. Steve? Brian? It doesn't matter; what matters, is that it puts me at 500. . . 500! I've racked up a lot of frequent dater points. That's all the more reason I'm holding tight to my guy, Ryne, and am determined to give him a Chanukah present that'll knock his tallis off.

The good news is, this year I don't have to hustle. When Ryne and I were doing the just-friends thing, he mentioned he wanted a new chai to wear around his neck. Something about ripping his chain during a football game and losing his old one on the field. I knew we were a relationship waiting to happen, so I filed that nugget away in my mental vault. Actually I wrote it on a piece of paper, because I didn't want to forget. Of course then I forgot where I put the paper. But details. . . .

I know, I know, buying a chai may be a bit spendy; but I'm head over high heels for Ryne. I want to show him how much he means to me. I want to put it all out there. Lay it all on the line. No gifts, no glory, right?

So Ryne and I head to the jeweler's hand in hand. We pick a simple, classy, white gold chai. But before I can congratulate myself on a gift well done, our saleslady, Patrice, asks if we need a chain.

"I have a broken chain at home; I just need to fix it. I actually got it here when I got my old chai," answered Ryne.

Boyfriend said what? I didn't know he got his last chai here. From who? He didn't buy it for himself and his folks live out of town. So the only person who would have shopped here for him was . . .

"My ex, but that doesn't matter."

Doesn't matter? Doesn't matter! I thought my chai was a one-of-a-kind gift. I thought I was boldly going where no date had gone before. But no. Apparently *she* got him one. And now he wants to put my chai on her chain. You can't wear a gift from your new girlfriend on a chain from your old one. That chain is tarnished.

I don't even understand why he still has it. I don't want to make Mount Sinai out of a molehill, but this is a big deal. What else of hers did he keep? I bet she bought him that sweatshirt he's wearing. And those jeans. And that belt. Take them off now. Wow. Okay. Well, that worked out well for me. So does the story.

Driving home from the jeweler, Ryne finally gets it. "You're right, C. If the charm's from you and the chain's from her, the necklace would be a chai-brid."

That's when I lose it. In a good way. I'm laughing so hard I'm going to plotz. Did he just say chai-brid? Seriously? Chai-brid? Only Ryne could come up with that corny combo. Only Ryne could make me laugh this hard when I'm supposed to be mad. Only Ryne and I could have this much fun together.

That's when it hits me. He may have her chain, but I have his heart.

*Chanukah* means "dedicated." As in I'm getting Ryne an expensive gift because I'm dedicated to this relationship. But *Maccabee* means "hammer." As in, we still have a few relationship kinks to hammer out. But isn't that how we grow closer? So I did what any sexy Jewess would do. I bought him a new chain, one that looks way better on him than the other one. Which makes sense, since I'm way better for him than that other girl.

Lesson learned? A relationship's greater than the sum of its gifts. Well that, and the best way to motivate someone to buy you a gift is to tell them you're going to start wearing the one your ex gave you. If only I had an old diamond ring lying around.

......................................................

# THEY TRIED TO KILL US, WE WON, LET'S EAT

Ring or no diamond ring, Chanukah's a holiday that everyone can get down with. It's Chanukah, baby, Chanukah. What's not to love? There's no fasting, there's no guilt, just lots of latkes, presents, and fun. And hot Jewish hunks. The Chanukah story famously stars a strapping band of Jewish brothers:

## THE BIG MACS

In 168 BCE, Israel was ruled by this Syrian dude, King Antiochus. He said everyone should practice the same religion—his. This was a no-go for the Jews, especially Mattathias. Syrian soldiers ordered Matt to sacrifice a pig on an altar. Yeah, right. Mattathias opened up an ice-cold can of whoop tuchus on them. After delivering a severe beat-down, our buddy Matt and his five smoking-hot sons fled to the hills. They recruited a rag-tag gang of farmers and shepherds to join them in their fight. Have no fear, the 5'6" Jews are here. I'm sure the colossal Syrians were shaking in their sandals. Led by Matt's son Judah "the Hammer" Maccabee, this army of nice Jewish boys raged guerilla warfare on the Syrian military machine. And after three years, the Jews KO'd the Syrians and took back Jerusalem.

After doing a victory lap, the Macs got to the Temple to find the Syrians had trashed the place. There were beer cans and cigarette butts everywhere. And also statues of Zeus and a bunch of Greek shrine stuff. The Macs scrubbed the place spic and span, then rededicated the Temple, but they only found enough oil to re-light the *Ner Tamid* (eternal light) for one night. But—insert drumroll here—the oil lasted eight nights. Amazing, but kind of unnecessary. Seriously, how long does it take for a Maccabee to go on an olive oil run? If it was a beer run, he'd been back in five minutes. Man's inability to run errands aside, the oil's stamina is pretty impressive. Okay, fine, it's miraculous. Chanukah is a holiday of miracles.

- It's a miracle that Judah and his brothers really were in six-pack shape. Most guys just lie about it on JDate. Yeah, right, you're "athletic/fit."

- It's a miracle that a small team of Jewish fighters defeated a huge Syrian army. Jews always manage to prevail even in the most impossible situations. That includes you. You want to squeeze into your skinny jeans by Saturday night? It may seem impossible, but you can do it. Just don't lose faith. Or eat that latke. I said put down the fried carb.

- It's a miracle that my boyfriend got me the Judith Jack earrings I wanted for Chanukah. Or at least he will after reading this book. Babe, they're small marquisate earrings with a teardrop charm. The lady at the Nordstrom's jewelry counter will know which ones I mean.

- We learn that The Miracle of Chanukah totally trumps *Miracle on 34th Street*. A house? Really? Is that the best you've got, Santa?

## C'MON BABY, LIGHT MY FIRE

Speaking of the other holiday, while the goys are hanging Christmas lights, the Jews are lighting Chanukah candles—for eight nights. Take that, Clark Griswald. We light the menorah to give props to that long-lasting, overachieving olive oil. We also light the candles to remember the moral of the Chanukah story: you can't get rid of us that easily. The Jewish people are like a candle that refuses to go out. Or a guest that refuses to go home. And when we do go home, we take leftovers with us. God forbid a little food should go to waste.

## LIGHTING THE MENORAH

The Chanukah story teaches us that even in the darkest times, there's a light at the end of the menorah. Unless you don't know how to light a menorah, then you're in the dark. So let's review:

- Start with one candle in the menorah on the first night and add an additional candle every night. Be sure to load the candles from right to left and light the candles from left to right.

- On the first night, we say three blessings over the candles. For the next seven nights, we only say two. Why? After the first night, everyone wants to get to the presents as quickly as possible. Also, we only say the third blessing, Shehecheyanu, after performing a mitzvah (like lighting the Chanukah candles) for the first time that year.

- Don't use the candlelight for anything practical like reading a book, lighting a cig, or flipping though a magazine. Like supermodels, and me, the candles are meant to be admired for their beauty.

- Running low on gelt? Don't buy a spendy menorah. Make your own using the tea lights you bought at Bed Bath & Beyond ... with the $5 off $15 purchase coupon that came in the mail. Celebrate Chanukah and save money—it's a double mitzvah! If only it were double coupons.

- If you're doing the do-it-yourself route, remember eight isn't enough. A *Chanukiah* (Chanukah menorah) holds nine candles, one for each night plus the *shamas* (worker candle). And like a goy in a crowd of Jews, the shamas should stand taller than the rest.

- Don't use each candle to light the next; instead use the shamas to light all the others. Like a party-hopping fool, the shamas will go from candle to candle and make sure every one gets lit.

- After lighting the menorah, place it in the window. This lets Santa know you're a flyover house. It's also a public display of Jewish pride that lets everyone know you're celebrating Chanukah. And by everyone I mean the handsome lawyer in 3B. "In case you're wondering, the single woman in 3G is an M.O.T. Ask her out."

## CHANUKAH PRESENTS

The tradition of giving Chanukah gifts is fairly new, and in my opinion, fairly nice. There's nothing better than getting a Chanukah gift from your boyfriend . . . except getting a little blue box from Tiffany's. Or getting a little blue box from Tiffany's from your boyfriend. Yes, ladies, when it comes to gifts it's always better to receive than to give. No matter what those do-gooders say. So get in the spirit of the season and demand that your boyfriend give you eight gifts. Nine if you count the shamas.

If you expect your boy to buy you a gift, be prepared to buy one in return. How much gelt should you drop on your guy? The Jewish Dating Bureau advises that when purchasing a gift for your man spend around $10 to $15 for every month you've been together. If you've been casually dating for two months, spend $20 to $30. A gift in this range says "I'm thinking of you," not "You're all I think about." If you've been dating for six months, spend $60 to $90. A present at this price point says "We're going places." If you've been dating for a year spend $120 to $180. A gift in this range says, "This is serious, I love you . . . and I expect you to spend at least this much on me."

When shopping for your mensch, get him something memorable, something that makes you stand out. Buy your man surf lessons, concert tickets, or a weekend in Vegas with you. Or surprise him with a guys' night out combo pack complete with a gift card from his favorite steakhouse, a bottle of Johnnie Walker Black, and cab fare home from his night with friends. He'll love it and his buddies will give you mad props. Remember the whole point of giving a gift is to make yourself look good. And to get good gifts in return.

·············································································

# THROW A ROCKIN' ROCK OF AGES PARTY

Chanukah is a time for parents and children to come together, sing holiday songs, and play Spin the Dreidel. The only problem is that I'd rather play Spin the Bottle. You too? Then throw a raging Latkes 'n' Liquor party. I'm talking drunken dreidel, a rowdy gift exchange, and kissing-under-the-knisheltoe.

O Chanukah, O Chanukah come light the menorah

Have fun at my party, but don't be a whore-a

Gather round the table, there's hot boys to meet

Forget about your diet, there's latkes to eat

And while we are drinking and flirting on into the night,

We'll think of Judah, and eat some more food-ah

Until our new jeans feel tight

We'll think of Judah, get in a good mood-ah,

'Cuz this party's gonna be tight.

## D.U.I.–DREIDELING UNDER THE INFLUENCE

You can't host a happening Chanukah party without a down-and-dirty game of dreidel. There are four Hebrew letters engraved on the traditional dreidel: Nun, Gimel, Heh, and Shin. They stand for *Nes Gadol Haya Sham*, "a Great

Miracle Happened There." In Israel, they sport their own dreidel remix with the letters Nun, Gimel, Heh, and Peh, which stands for *Nes Gadol Haya Po*, "a Great Miracle Happened Here." Well, tonight, a great drinking game's happening here.

The rules are simple. Everyone starts with a glass of beer. Each guest spins the dreidel and then drinks according to where it lands. If the dreidel lands on:

- **Nun: the guest drinks nothing**
- **Gimel: the guest pounds the whole glass**
- **Heh: the guest chugs half the glass**
- **Shin/Peh: the guest buys a round**

For the lightweights: Gimel drinks eight sips, Heh drinks four.

Bonus round: replace the beer with shots. Same rules apply. Just keep an eye on your guests. Friends don't let friends dreidel and drive.

## CHANUKAH GRUB

It's not a Jew party unless you've got Jew food. So what's a Jewish babe like you supposed to serve? Fried food, fake coins, and chocolate chip cheesecake.

**LATKES AND SUFGANIYOT:** Time to make the donuts . . . and latkes. Why do we eat fried foods on Chanukah? To celebrate that whole miraculous oil thing. Also, the great rabbis knew that if people got drunk playing dreidel they'd start craving something greasy. So uphold a longstanding Jewish tradition and soak up that alcohol with a *schmaltzy* (greasy) feast. Throw a few *sufganiyot* (donuts) in the deep fryer and whip up some homemade couch potato *latkes* (see recipe). Of course, you can also stop at Dunkin' Donuts for a dozen sufganiyot and buy prepackaged frozen potato pancakes at the store. Your friends will be too farshikkert to know the difference, and you can spend that extra time bagging yourself a Maccabee.

**CHANUKAH GELT:** I love the smell of latkes in the morning. But for your buzzed guests who prefer to chow down on chocolate, serve up those little bags of chocolate Chanukah *gelt* (money). Why do Jews eat fake gold coins? They're a playful take on the tradition of giving real Chanukah gelt. The victorious Maccabees minted new coins as a sign of freedom and gave them out to teachers, children, and the poor. Eventually, the coins became gifts, the children became everyone, and that's how I got my new earrings. Thanks again, honey.

**CHEESECAKE:** A lesser-known Chanukah tradition is serving cheesecake in honor of Judith, a Chanukah heroine with real chutzpah. In the time of the Maccabees, a Syrian general named Holofernes decided to kill all the Jews in the village of Berhulia. Women, children, even alter kockers. So this shayna maidel, Judith, slithered into her sexiest toga, threw on her "come schtup me" sandals, and packed a picnic basket filled with bottles of wine and salty cheese—Jews don't go anywhere without a little nosh. Then Judith made a run for the Syrian camp. Holofernes was floored by this Hebrew hottie. And she brought food? Score! He invited her to stay and check out his fish tank. Judith fed the general salty cheese until he got thirsty, then poured him wine until he passed out. Once he was down for the count, sweet, sexy Judith pulled a sword out of her picnic basket, beheaded Holo, and threw his severed keppe in the basket. Talk about giving head! She returned to Bethulia, planted his head on a stake, and scared away the rest of Holo's army. It may take a village to raise a child, but it takes a woman to save a village. Now we eat cheesecake to celebrate Judith and her salty cheese. Hungry?

## THE MAGNIFICENT SEVEN

You served the right food, you schooled your friends in dreidel, and your Latkes 'n' Liquor party was a huge success. Great—but what are you supposed to do for the other seven nights? If you're multi-dating, Chanukah's your holiday. You don't have to choose which guy to spend the holiday with; you just have to choose which night of the holiday to spend with which guy. Spend night one with Adam, night two with Jordan, night three with Eddie, and so on. Mattathias had five sons, so it only seems appropriate that you have five dates.

Then spend at least one night of Chanukah participating in the ancient Jewish tradition of picking up Chinese food. Why are we eating with chopsticks? Like most men, the Maccabees were too lazy to cook dinner for themselves, so they ordered in from Fu's Palace. Also, Christmas usually falls sometime during Chanukah, and Chinese restaurants are often the only ones open on Christmas Day. That explains why Jews often celebrate night number six by ordering a number twenty-six.

Oy to the world! Another Chanukah tradition is going to a giant Jewish singles' party—on Christmas Eve. 'Twas the fourth night of Chanukah, and all through the house, the single Jews were partying, so who needs a spouse? In every city, crowds of young Heebs get together to party their tuchuses off while their goyish counterparts are stuck home hanging stockings. What else is a Jew supposed to do? These events carry a slightly steep cover charge ($50 to $75), attract Jews ages 21 to 40, and are held in large bars, clubs, and hotel ballrooms. They all have names like The Matzo Ball, Knishmas, or The Latkepalooza. But they should have names like In The Bag, The Done Deal, or The Sure Thing. There are hundreds of desperate Jews, an open bar, and the Adam Sandler Chanukah Song playing on a loop. Believe me—it won't take a miracle for you to take someone home.

# COUCH POTATO LATKES RECIPE

Too lazy to *potchkeh* (fuss) in the kitchen? These latkes are super-simple to make. And super cheap. You can whip up the whole recipe for under $5 and spend the gelt you saved on a sexy new halter dress. The latkes shouldn't be the only hot little things at your party.

MAKES ABOUT 18 LATKES

2 LARGE RUSSET POTATOES

2 TABLESPOONS VEGETABLE OIL

1 LARGE YELLOW ONION

2 EGGS

¼ CUP MATZO MEAL

A BISSEL OF SALT (ABOUT 1 TEASPOON)

A BISSEL OF PEPPER (ABOUT 1 TEASPOON)

Peel and grate the potatoes. You can grate them by hand or toss them in a food processor with the grating attachment. If you're single and haven't registered for a food processor (and seriously, who buys their own Cuisinart?), you can buy a bag of already grated potatoes at the store.

Place the shredded potatoes in a colander set over a bowl and gently press out the excess liquid with the palm of your hand. The less liquid in your mixture, the crispier the latkes. Guys like girls with crispy latkes, know what I'm saying? No? Neither do I. But it sounded sexy.

Heat the oil in a nonstick skillet. While the oil is heating, peel and grate the onion.

Throw everything into one large bowl: potatoes, onion, eggs, matzo meal, salt, and pepper.

When the oil is hot, really hot, Abercrombie-and-Fitch-model hot, carefully drop the batter in the pan about ¼-cup at a time, cooking in batches if necessary. Flatten it with a spatula; the latkes should be about 2½ inches wide.

Cook about 3 to 4 minutes on each side, turning once, until they turn golden-brown—about the color of your highlighted hair. Set the finished latkes on a plate covered with a layer of paper towel to cool slightly.

**TIPS:**

- Don't buy little-pisher-sized potatoes. They're a pain in the tuchus to peel.
- You want to get your shredded raw potato mixture cooking as quickly as possible; the exposure to the air will turn the potatoes green. And green pancakes don't look appetizing. Plus green and red are the other team's colors.
- Transfer your cooked latkes onto paper towels; they act like super-sized blotting sheets that soak up excess oil.
- Latkes can be cooked earlier in the day and reheated. Place them on baking sheets covered with parchment paper, and heat them up at 350° F for a few minutes.

# CHAPTER 11

# LITTLE MISS SHUSHAN
## (PURIM)

Last month my friend Renee invited me to the giant Pour 'Em on Purim party at her synagogue. I threw on my best pupik-baring costume and claimed I never missed a good Megillah. I also never missed a chance to flirt with some nice Jewish boys when I looked come-schtup-me hot. And believe me, I looked crazy-svelte. I wore an itsy bitsy teeny weeny leaf-covered bikini, a mini sarong skirt, a rubber snake, and stilettos. One look at me dressed as Eve, and those boys would be begging me to partake of their fruit.

We pulled up to the synagogue around seven, and the joint was jam-packed. The sanctuary was a sea of sequins, feathers, masks, and a lot of girls dressed like Esther. If Esther was working the corner of Shushan and Sunset. There were also plenty of good-looking guys; like Andy, who I met in line for the bar. A rare 6' 2" Jew, he was a little bit slick and a little bit schmaltzy, which for some reason I found a little bit sexy. He was also a little bit tipsy; okay, fine, he was totally farshikkert. But it was Purim, everyone in Shushan was getting sloshed. Besides, he was fun to talk to. In the ten minutes it took to get our drinks, I learned he was a lawyer, he was hilarious, and he had the most amazing green eyes. I liked this guy. Something about him had a hold on me. And I'm not just talking about his right hand on my tush, although I think I felt him grab it.

The next Saturday night, Andy and I stepped out on our first official date. He wowed me with an impossible-to-get reservation at a star-studded sushi spot in Hollywood. A table at this place was more coveted than a neighbor's hot wife; I'll admit I was impressed. And not just by his pull with the maître 'd. Andy was charming and handsome, and the date was going great. We were debating what to order next, albacore sashimi or a spicy tuna roll, when Andy said, "It's funny, you look so different than you did on Purim."

I'm sorry, what? Did he just say I looked different? And he called it funny? Well, it better be hilarious that I'm even more stunning than he remembered.

"But maybe that's because I was really drunk on Purim," he finished.

And there it was, the old drunk-on-Purim excuse. On Purim, Jews are commanded to drink until we can't tell blessed Mordechai from wicked Haman, the good from the bad, the hot from the not. Yes, right up there with thou shall not kill and thou shall feed the hungry is thou shall get lit up to the point of poor judgment on Purim. Well, clearly the ancient rabbis knew nothing about the love life of the modern Jewish man. They don't need hamantaschen, a holiday, and Talmudic incentive to get drunk and toss on beer goggles. Jewish men do that just fine all on their own, thank you very much. They do it every Saturday night without instruction. In fact, by the time Purim rolls around, Jewish guys have to step their game up if they want to fulfill the commandment. They literally drink until they can't tell the difference between a *shayna maidel* (pretty girl) and *zaftig mieskeit* (plump, ugly girl). . . .

"Wait, how different?" I asked Andy. I couldn't look that different. Costume or street clothes, drunk or not, I'm a good catch. There were more than a few sober men at that Purim party that wanted to spin me like a graggor.

"Don't get all sensitive," he said. "All I meant was that when a girl rocks a costume the way you did, it's hard to get that image out of your head. You looked so gorgeous the other night, and you look good now, but—"

But? Did he just say "but"? I don't need a man who says "but" after the words "you look good." You look good, period. The sentence should have ended there. He didn't have to explain that I looked sexier last time. That he's disappointed I wore something in public that actually covered my pupik. What's next? "I was going to pay for dinner, but" or "I love you, but" or "I do, but."

*Purim* means "lots," and there will be lots of times in a relationship when my man won't be Purim-level inebriated and I won't look quite as come-hither hot. I mean, I'll always look hot, just not as hot. Sometimes you have a bad hair day, or it's laundry day, or he sees you when you first wake up in the morning. Not that I know anything about that, I just heard. . . . My point is I need a man who's going to love me no matter what. Hot, not, glasses, contacts, jeans, or lingerie. Someone who spends our first date noticing I'm more incredible than he imagined, not more covered than he recalled.

On Purim we may drink until we can't tell the good guys from the bad guys, but I don't need Esther, a costume, and a triangle cookie to tell a good date from a bad date. I can do that just fine all on my own, thank you very much. And yes, the restaurant was amazing, and Andy was definitely a funny, successful, good-looking, guy but . . .

## MEGILLAH MADNESS

I didn't let my date with Andy ruin my love of Purim; in fact, that'd be impossible. You can't have a bad time on Purim. Purim is the party of the year. It's Jews Gone Wild. It's a total let-loose, good times, get-drunk rager. So gather up your friends, get out the keg, and get ready to Shushan it up. With all the masks, feathers, drinking, dancing, carnivals, and parades, Purim is like a circumcised Mardi Gras. And yes, I'll flash for graggors.

# THE WHOLE MEGILLAH

Every Adar, families, singletons, and partygoers gather around to hear the *Megillah* (the story of Esther) read aloud from the single scroll it's written on. With drunk congregants, loud noisemakers, and a footloose attitude, it's the most raucous and rowdy reading of the year. Here's what they show up to hear:

In the land of Shushan, King Ahasverus and his boys were kicking it at the palace; drinking Scotch, eating pizza, and watching the game on his giant flat-screen rock. Ahasverus drunk-dialed his wife, Vashti, and ordered her to come down and do a pole dance for his posse. He wanted to show off her sexy body to his buds. Vashti told Ahasverus to schtup off. Ahasverus told Vashti to get out.

Naturally, the only thing Ahasverus could do was hold a beauty pageant to find a new queen. Mordechai convinced his cousin Esther to sign up. Good thing, too. She owned the swimsuit competition, rocked her Valentino evening gown, and stole the talent portion with her Hava Negilah. Our shayna maidel Esther was crowned Little Miss Shushan; she just hoped that no one discovered her Jewish roots. Or those nude photos.

Now the King's sidekick, Haman, was stark-raving meshugenne. This wicked schmuck convinced Ach to sign a decree to kill all the Jews. When Mordechai heard of the plot, he begged Esther to talk to the King and save the Jews from the evil Darth Haman. "This is our most desperate hour. Help us, Esther-wan, you're our only hope."

But King Ahasverus took "Don't call me, I'll call you" to a whole new level. If you showed up at his crib uninvited, he'd kill you. Gulp. Esther knew she had to put her best high heel forward. She fasted for three days, squeezed into her tightest royal robe, and made an unannounced booty call. Esther looked so stunning that Ach wasn't mad at her for crashing. He was actually excited to see her. So excited that he held out his golden scepter for Esther to touch. She rubbed it, and next thing you know, a satisfied King said he'd do whatever Esther wanted. She wanted him and his buddy Haman to come to her big banquet. Once both men were full and drunk, Esther revealed her secret Heeb identity, exposed Haman, and saved the Jews of Shushan. In a last-minute trade, the King dropped Haman and picked up Mordechai. Then ordered that Haman be hanged from the gallows he built for the Jews.

What do we learn from our heroine Esther?

- You can't *schmy* (meander) around all day waiting for God (who's not even mentioned in the Megillah) to help you. You need to make like Esther and pull yourself up by your own Kenneth Cole bootstraps.
- Sometimes you have to put out to help out.
- It's important to give good scepter.

· · · · · · · · · · · · · · · · · · · · · · · · · · · · · · · · · · · · · · · · · · · · · · · · · · · · · ·

# THE NEW JEW REVUE

Different from your typical night at temple, the Megillah reading is a real three-ring service. To start, every time the reader says the name Haman, congregants drown out the sound of it with *graggors* (noisemakers), trumpets, whistles, drums, and—for those sad little kids with no noisemakers—booing. Haman was so evil that Jews don't even want to hear his name mentioned. Haman was the original He Who Should Not Be Named. Or at least the original He Whose Name Should Not Be Heard.

## WHO WAS THAT MASKED JEW?

To add to the chaos, Jews wear costumes to the Megillah reading. What's with the masquerade madness? Esther hid her Jewish identity from the King, so Jews hide their true identity from each other. Plus, costumes automatically up the fun factor.

Now, the modern Jewish babe fasts the day before Purim so she looks as svelte as possible in her poulke-showing, pupik-baring costume. Well, also to honor Esther's three-day fast. But let's get back to the pupik-baring and poulke-showing. As a young girl, you dressed up as old standbys like Esther and Vashti. As a trendy yenta, you should dress up as new standbys, like naughty Esther and sexy Vashti. Actually, anything goes on Purim, so feel free to ditch the Shushan-themed costumes altogether and come dressed as a French maid, a high-school cheerleader, or a hot librarian. Go as Princess Leia in her slave bikini or a naughty Jewish shul girl in a miniskirt. The less clothing the better— Esther had it going on and so should you. Don't wait until October to tempt those nice Jewish boys with your barely there costume. Remember, the whole point of dressing up is to end up hooking up.

## THE WHOLE SPIEL

To pump up the Purim merriment even more, we throw giant carnivals, stage big parades, perform silly *spiels* (plays), give comedic roasts, and play practical jokes on one another. So feel free stage a spoof, make fun of friends, and bring the funny. Yes, funny like a clown. Purim is often called the Jewish Halloween, so think of the spiels as Schtick-or-Treat.

Is this a joke? Some people think so. Many Jews believe Purim isn't just about playing practical jokes; it is a practical joke. The whole thing's a farce, a made-up tale, an improbable bubbe maiseh that you'd have to be drunk to believe. Good thing most of us are.

## L'CHAIM

Purim means "lots," as in Haman drew lots to decide which day he'd kill us on. Of course, "lots" could also refer to the amount of alcohol Jews drink on Purim. Congregants bring bottles to the bimah and keep flasks in their bags. Don't judge—these drunken Jews are just following the Talmud's orders. As you learned from Andy, on Purim, we're commanded to booze until we can't tell blessed Mordechai from wicked Haman, the hero from the villain, the schmoozers from the losers. In Hebrew it's called *Adloyada*. In dating it's called Purim-goggles.

# GREAT, WE SURVIVED . . . I'M STARVING

Purim's definitely a big drinking day, but it's also a big eating day. The Megillah tells us to celebrate the holiday with feasts and days of gladness, so Purim parties have a spread that rivals Esther's banquet. There's no specific menu mapped out; if you're throwing a Purim party, serve up whatever sounds good. Or whatever you can cook well. Or order in well. Esther was a Jewish Princess; you think she actually cooked that big banquet herself? Please, her royal chefs whipped it up for her. So make like Esther and make it easy on yourself. Call your local deli and pick up a couple trays of corned beef, pastrami, chopped liver, and salami—also known as the Jew-plate special.

## HAMANTIME

Let's talk dessert. Nothing says Purim like a hamantaschen. Except a knockout drunk girl dressed as Vashti. But enough about me, let's get back to the cookie. This holiday treat can't be beat. It's sweet, irresistible, and a little flaky. But again, that's enough about me. A *hamantaschen* is a triangle-shaped cookie that's filled in the middle with strawberry, raspberry, apricot, chocolate, apple, prune, *mun* (poppy seed), or whatever flavor you like. And who doesn't like to get their hamantaschen stuffed?

The hamantaschen's triangle shape is a nod to Haman's three-cornered hat. It's also a celebration of Esther's girl power. The triangle is a symbol for female, and it was a woman who saved the day. That's a little subtle, don't you think? If we're going to honor Esther's womanly strength, we should do more than give her an isosceles cookie. We should rent a Jumbotron or give her a T-shirt–ready catchphrase—something like "Who needs a hero when we have a she-ro," or "Girls kick tuchus." Or my favorite: "This princess saves herself."

# THANKS FOR SHARING

Whatever the reason behind their triangle shape, it's important to share your hamantaschen with others. Why? All those calories will go straight to your poulkes. Also, Purim is a time when Jews perform the mitzvah of sharing food with others. With *matanot l'evyonim* (gifts to the poor), we donate at least enough tzedakah to feed two poor people a full meal. I'm talking appetizers, soup, salad, entrée, dessert, coffee, fruit plate, cheese plate, even that little sorbet palate-cleansing course. The idea is that everyone, even the poor, should be able to enjoy a huge Purim feast.

Purim is also a time to *shalach manot* (send portions) to friends. We fill small gift baskets with all kinds of nosherai: hamantaschen, wine, nuts, sweets, fruit, and the occasional regifted Bing cherry chocolates that were leftover from the Harry and David basket that your co-workers gave you for the holidays. Not that I would ever do that. If my colleagues are reading this, I ate all those Bing cherry chocolates myself.

Borrowing from a Christmas tradition, go-getting Martha Stewart types bake dozens of their favorite cookies, then get together and swap basket-filling sweets at a Great Purim Cookie Exchange. That sounds good in theory, but none of the young Jewish women I know are Martha Stewart types. When was the last time you ate a waffle that wasn't frozen? Or made your own potpourri? Or even used potpourri? Exactly, that's why I participate in the Great Purim Cookie Buy. I go to the kosher bakery, buy a few dozen cookies, and toss them in some baskets. If I have baskets. Usually you're looking at a paper plate with some foil over it. Happy Purim!

# HAMANTASCHEN

Haman may have been a bad man, but hamantaschen are a great dessert. These simple, delicious cookies take minutes to make, but masquerade as something much more difficult. Between your sexy costume and your sweet cookies, you'll be picking up a Purim date in no time.

MAKES APPROXIMATELY 24 COOKIES

2 TABLESPOONS MILK

1 STICK (4 OUNCES) BUTTER OR MARGARINE

1 EGG

1 TEASPOON VANILLA

1 CUP SUGAR

2 TEASPOONS BAKING POWDER

2 CUPS FLOUR, SIFTED

FILLING OF CHOICE (1 JAR OF KOSHER PRESERVES OR 1 CAN OF KOSHER FRUIT OR POPPY SEED PIE FILLING)

Mix milk, butter, egg, vanilla, and sugar in large bowl.

Add baking powder and flour; stir.

Preheat oven to 350°F.

On a floured surface, roll dough out to ¼-inch thick. While rolling, decide what sexy character you'll dress up as tonight.

Use the rim of a glass to cut circles from the dough.

Place 1 spoonful of filling onto each circle, and fold edges to form a triangle. Pinch all three corners to seal. Set the cookies on a parchment-covered or greased cookie sheet.

Bake for 15 minutes. While waiting, fill the glass with a cocktail and start your Purim preparty.

Serve cookies while looking stunning.

**TIPS:**

- Fill hamantaschen with your favorite flavor (strawberry, raspberry, apricot, chocolate, apple, prune, or poppy seed pie) or alternate flavors for a combo pack.
- If you want to make pareve hamantaschen, use pareve margarine and substitute 2 tablespoons of water or orange juice for the 2 tablespoons of milk.

••••••••••••••••••••••••••••••••••••••••••••••••••••••••••••••••••••••

# POUR 'EM ON PURIM

Throwing a Purim party? Observe the commandment to drink up a few of these classic Jewish cocktails.

••••••••••••••••••••••••••••••••••••••••••••••••••••••••••••••••••••••

## BIMAH COLADA
### A Piña Colada from a higher authority.

2 OUNCES PINEAPPLE JUICE

1 OUNCE CREAM OF COCONUT

1½ OUNCES LIGHT OR DARK RUM

½ CUP ICE CUBES

WHIPPED CREAM, FOR SERVING

PINEAPPLE WEDGE, FOR SERVING

MARASCHINO CHERRY, FOR SERVING

Combine in a blender for 30 seconds. Top with whipped cream, a pineapple wedge, and a cherry. If you like Bimah Coladas and getting caught in the rain . . .

# COSMOTPOLITAN
**Drink of young yentas everywhere.**

SUGAR, FOR THE COCKTAIL GLASS
2 OUNCES VODKA
1 OUNCE TRIPLE SEC
2 OUNCES CRANBERRY JUICE
½ OUNCE FRESH LIME JUICE

Rim the glass with sugar. Shake the ingredients together with ice, strain into a martini glass, and gossip with your girls about your bad blind date.

........................................................................................................

# DIN & TONIC
**Gin and tonic you drink while debating Jewish law.**

3 OUNCES GIN
6 OUNCES TONIC WATER
LIME, FOR SERVING

Combine the gin and tonic in a glass. Throw in a lime. Get a good buzz while proving your point.

........................................................................................................

# FRUM & COKE
**For the observant Jew.**

3 OUNCES DARK RUM
6 OUNCES COKE
ICE, FOR SERVING
LIME, FOR SERVING

Combine in a glass over ice. Garnish with a lime. Flirt away.

# FUZZY PUPIK

**A fuzzy navel made by a Jewish girl with great abs.**

2 OUNCES VODKA

1 OUNCE PEACH SCHNAPPS

4 OUNCES ORANGE JUICE

Shake ingredients together, pour into a glass, and drink while flaunting your flat stomach.

---

# JEW-DRIVER

**A fun way to get your full day's supply of vitamin C.**

4 OUNCES ORANGE JUICE

2 OUNCES VODKA

ICE, FOR SERVING

Mix, stir, drink.

---

# MACHER-ITA

**A margarita made by a big shot.**

SALT, FOR THE COCKTAIL GLASS

1 OUNCE TEQUILA

3 OUNCES MARGARITA MIX

The modern Jewish babe doesn't have time to futz around with triple sec and lime juice. So buy a premade mix, blend, and enjoy.

## MINT JEW-LUP
### A Jewish take on a Kentucky Derby classic.

1 OUNCE SIMPLE SYRUP
3 OUNCES BOURBON
8 SPRIGS FRESH MINT
CRUSHED ICE, FOR SERVING

Muddle six mint sprigs into simple syrup. Pour into a frosted glass packed with ice, add the bourbon. Garnish with mint and a straw, and drink while modeling an oversized Derby kippah.

----

## MIMOSHE
### The Mimosa Moshe drank while wandering the desert.

3 OUNCES ORANGE JUICE
3 OUNCES CHAMPAGNE

Combine in a chilled champagne glass. Drink with lox-and-bagel brunch.

----

## MOTINI
### For the suave Members of the Tribe.

2 OUNCES GIN OR VODKA
¼ OUNCE DRY VERMOUTH
ICE, FOR SERVING

Shake or stir with ice, and strain into a chilled martini glass. Olives or lemon twist are optional. Attitude isn't.

## SCHMUTZIDIK MOTINI
**For the dirty Jew.**

Add ½ ounce olive juice to your MOTini before you shake or stir with ice, and strain into a chilled martini glass. Garnish with olives and dirty thoughts.

........................................................................................................

## SCHTUP ON THE BEACH
**For a little fun in the sun.**

**2 OUNCES VODKA**

**2 OUNCES PEACH SCHNAPPS**

**2 OUNCES ORANGE JUICE**

**2 OUNCES CRANBERRY JUICE**

Stir briefly, pour over ice, and run your toes through the sand.

........................................................................................................

## SEVEN AND SEVEN AND SEVEN
**A Seven and Seven that you drink on Shabbat.**

**2 OUNCES SEAGRAM'S 7 WHISKEY**

**4 OUNCES 7-UP**

Pour Seagram's and 7-Up over ice. Kick-start your day of rest.

# TEFILAH SUNRISE

**A tequila sunrise drunk after a morning minyan.**

2 OUNCES TEQUILA

1 OUNCE GRENADINE

4 OUNCES ORANGE JUICE

MARASCHINO CHERRY, FOR SERVING

Pour the tequila over ice. Slowly add a layer of grenadine. Gently pour a layer of OJ on top. Drop a maraschino cherry in the glass. To achieve that sunrise-sunset look, try to keep the layers like an Orthodox service—separated.

---

# MANISCHEWITZ WITH A CHALLAH CHASER

**The traditional Shabbos drink.**

Pour Manischewitz into a wineglass. Say Kiddush. Drink. Say Hamotzi. Eat.

# CHAPTER 12

# HOW TO LOSE A GUY IN TEN PLAGUES
## (PASSOVER)

This Pesach I'm celebrating more than our Exodus from Egypt. I'm celebrating my Exodus from online dating. I'm breaking free from the bonds of blind dates. This Passover is all about what God did for me when I came forth out of the dating pool.

What's matzah brei and Adir Hu have to do with who I'm dating? Everything, ladies, everything. My guy Ben and I have been doing the casual dating thing for three months. So far, so great. Ben has a quick wit, a kind heart, and I've got no complaints in the shank bone department. But I'm starting to crave more commitment. That little voice—well, not so little: that would imply that I have the ability to keep my volume down, which I don't. I talk quickly, I talk loudly, and I talk a lot, so let's say that *big* voice inside my heart is telling me to step things up.

That's where Passover comes into play. A holiday is a going-steady springboard. It's the perfect opportunity to push your relationship forward, and you've got to take advantage. Ask not what you're doing for the holiday, but what the holiday can do for you.

A week before Passover, I mention making holiday dinner for Ben.

"I thought I could make you my mom's world-famous matzah lasagna," I say. "She makes it every Passover—it's the best."

"You mean matzagna?" Ben asks. "If you're talking matzagna, I make the best."

Oh no, he didn't. He didn't just claim that he can keep up with my mom's lasagna. And he didn't just call it matzagna. That takes chutzpah. Those are fighting words. He's looking for a Passover culinary beat-down. Wait, that's it! Of course! Passover! Pesach's the perfect next step to bring us closer.

"No way is your lasagna better than mine," I argue. "I'm challenging you to Iron Chef: Matzah Lasagna."

"It's called matzagna—and it's on," he says.

"Like Moses in Egyptland, you're going down," I fire back.

Yes! Relationship, here we come. Ben and I aren't ready to head home together for Pesach. We aren't even ready to share a Seder. But a matzah throw-down? It's a holiday hangout without the holiday stress. No parents, no plane, no pressure. Just fun. We can skip the Four Questions and go straight to the four glasses. And then to the four times. My plan is foolproof.

We invite a dozen-plus friends to our Saturday-night showdown, so they can decide the winner. Let all who are hungry come and eat. And judge.

Tonight's Iron Chef Battle features Carin "the Feisty Balabusta" Davis versus Ben "the Mensch" Goldberg. Okay, Jews, I want a good fight, I want a clean fight. Every ingredient needs to carry a kosher l'Pesach hechsher, meals must be milchig, and both chefs have one hour.

It's go time. I'm mixing and measuring and layering and tasting. Where's the garlic? Is that enough sauce? Who moved my cheese? The kitchen is chaos. The cooking's intense. I'm running around like a kosher chicken with its keppe cut off.

We're both scrambling around for ingredients. I go old school: Streit's matzah, Miller's mozzarella, Rokeach tomato sauce, boom. He has all kinds of chazzerai on his side. He's roasting veggies, has four kinds of cheese, and what is that, eggplant? It doesn't matter. I can stand the heat; I'm not getting out of the kitchen.

As time runs out, our finished lasagnas are as different as we are. His is Wolfgang Puck and mine's Original Ray's. His is Reform and mine's traditional. His is Jewish fusion and mine's, well, better. At least I think so. But our friends don't. They call it a tie, claiming both are magically delicious. That's okay; even though I didn't win the game, I covered the relationship spread. And that was my real goal. Our matzah lasagna party was a huge hit, and hosting it together was a huge step. Our first joint holiday celebration. Next year in Jerusalem. Or Italy!

Thanks to our Passover cook-off, Ben and I have gone from dating to couple in one holiday. He calls all the time, he introduces me as his girlfriend, he even bought me a giant bouquet of sunflowers today. No, I haven't seen them yet, but I went hiking with Lisa, yenta is she, who talked to a friend, who talked to Brie, who works with Jen, who drank with Michael, who golfs with Fred, who lives with Ed, who owns the store which sold the flowers that my boychik bought for two zuzim. Had Gadya, Had Gadya.

●●●●●●●●●●●●●●●●●●●●●●●●●●●●●●●●●●●●●●●●●●●●●●●●●●●●●●●●●●●●

# THE PASSOVER STORY

You've now heard the Passover story of how I was freed from the chains of singlehood. At the Seder, you'll hear the Passover story of how Jews were freed from the chains of slavery. Passover is a celebration of those brave slaves who fled without bread. We celebrate them in three ways: We avoid eating *chametz* (leavened food), we actively eat *matzah* (unleavened bread), and we retell the Passover story at a Seder. Cue it up, boys:

## THE PASSOVER BUBBE MAISEH

Once we were slaves in Egypt. To add to our tsouris, this meshuggene Pharaoh declared that all Jewish newborn boys should be drowned in the Nile. But

Moses' mom couldn't send her son to swim with the fishes. Instead, she stuck her baby in a basket and sent him down the river . . . because that's better parenting. Pharaoh's daughter saw Moses floating by, took one look at his cute punim, and kept him for herself. Mo grew up in the palace, but eventually bailed town, became a shepherd, and struck up a conversation with a chatty burning bush. Through that flaming foliage, God told Mo to get his tuchus back to Egypt and save the Jews from slavery.

Moses asked Pharaoh to do him a solid, "Let my people go."

Pharaoh said, "No, no, no, I will not let them go."

"No? Then I'll huff and I'll puff and blow your pyramid in," said God.

Okay, God didn't puff. Or inhale. But he did bring down the hammer. And ten plagues. Before the last one, God told the Jews to mark their doors so the Angel of Death knew which homes to *posach* (pass over). That was considerate, but seriously, God, you're the All-knowing. Shouldn't you already know where your peeps are living? No wonder we got lost in the desert.

After the tenth plague, Pharaoh caved and kicked us out. It was a special, one-time-only offer, so we had to act now. We grabbed some crackers to nosh on and ran as fast as unathletic people can. Three days later Pharaoh wanted us back. He sent a whole army to hunt us down. But God parted the Red Sea, we crossed, and Pharaoh's folks didn't. Charlton Heston was nominated for a Golden Globe, and we're here to tell the tale and make fried matzah. Lessons learned:

- Like Pharaoh, it takes most men three days to realize they don't know what they got till it's gone.
- A bush can be a powerful thing.
- Why do people waste good money buying their kids designer strollers, Pack 'n' Plays, and Baby Bjorns? Moses went down the river with nothing but a basket under his backside, and he turned out okay.

# THE SEDER TABLE

Most people spend Passover Seder with their families. But your Pharaoh of a boss is making you work all week, so you can't go home for the holiday. Don't get all ferklempt. It's going to be okay. Worse things have happened, like slavery and bad hair days.

You can still get your Seder on. During Passover we're told to let all who are hungry come and eat; so we open our homes, Seders, and refrigerators to others. If you don't receive a personal invite, most synagogues, Hillels, and Jewish service groups host community Seders or arrange for in-home matches—which are like blind dates with someone else's crazy mishpacha.

Don't want to Seder with strangers? Then host a potluck Seder at your pad. You, your friends, your friends with benefits, and your friends you wished had benefits, can all get sloshed and full in the comfort of your own one-bedroom. That's right, on Passover we don't go to synagogue; we go to our kitchen table. Your kitchen table—that thing that's covered with old magazines, overdue bills, and miscellaneous junk mail. Yes, that thing. You can sit around that table and retell the Passover story. All you need are a few Passover props like Elijah's cup, a matzah tray, a Seder plate, some throw pillows, and Haggadot.

## MATZAH TRAY

This holiday I'm not the only thing that's flat. In honor of our ancestors' great escape, we eat matzah instead of bread. During the Seder, we spotlight three pieces of matzah in the matzah tray. They represent the three Jewish forefathers, Abe, Ike, and Jake; the three Jewish tribes, Cohen, Levi, and Israel; and the three Jewish stooges, Larry, Curly, and Moe.

If you own a fancy matzah tray from Israel, that's fab. If you still have the scribbled-upon matzah cover you made in Sunday school—great. If not, don't spend your cubicle-earned change on expensive Passover paraphernalia. Why buy it, when you can register for it . . . eventually. Until then, use any old non-chametzed plate and cover it with a napkin, a Burberry scarf, or a rally towel.

# ELIJAH'S CUP

Jews believe Elijah the Prophet's appearance will signal the coming of the Messianic Era. So during the Seder, we open our doors to welcome him and set out an extra glass of wine to serve him, just in case he stops by. God forbid a Jewish hostess runs out of food or is a place setting short, oy!

# THE SEDER PLATE

Don't own a fancy Seder plate with pretty pictures of plagues? Don't worry. Our ancestors didn't schlep through the desert with silver platters on their backs; so use whatever you've got that's chametz-free: a sectional veggie and dip dish, a glass tray, even a paper plate. It doesn't matter how much you spend on it; it just matters what you place on it—*karpas* (greens), *maror* (bitter herbs), *charoset*, a *beitzah* (roasted egg), and a *z'roah* (roasted shankbone).

I'll break down most of these items during the Seder section, but for now, know that the z'roah and beitzah symbolize festival offerings made at the Temple in Jerusalem. With the Temple destroyed, we no longer sacrifice animals; we just burn an egg and a shankbone. Of course, I also manage to burn my kugel, my kishke, and several other Seder dishes. . . .

# BETWEEN TWO PILLOWS . . .

The Seder is so long and dull that the hostess provides pillows for her guests to nod off on. Okay, that's not why they're there, but that's usually what happens. We actually lounge on pillows because in ancient Egypt reclining was the sign of a free man. So sit on it, Potsie.

# THE HAGGADAH

A *Haggadah*, which means "telling," is a book that recounts the Passover story. Haggadot come in all shapes, sizes, and lengths: feminist, modern, traditional, Hebrew, English, kids, illustrated. My family uses the free Maxwell House Haggadot they give away at the grocery store. Who knew that our ancestors grabbed both matzah and instant coffee on their way out the door?

······················································································

# THE PASSOVER SEDER

Your friends all agree to pop over to your place for Passover. Great, except you're not actually sure how to host a Seder. Don't fret, the Haggadah has your back. Like *An Idiot's Guide to Seders*, the Haggadah is a step-by-step manual to throwing a Passover party. And it doesn't matter which Haggadah you use, they all give the same play-by-play directions for the Seder. Our ancient, anal-retentive rabbis wanted to ensure that all Jews everywhere performed the *Seder*, which means "order," in the exact order they prescribed. So much for our freedom. Like the Seder itself, my explanation of that set order is a little long. So feel free to chug four glasses of wine while reading this next section.

**CANDLE LIGHTING**: Seder kicks off with a blessing over the candles. Not exactly what you had in mind when your date mentioned candlelight dinner, but you'll take it.

**KADESH**: This blessing introduces the first of the four, yes four, mandatory glasses of wine that we down during the Seder. They represent the four-fold promise God made to our ancestors in Egypt, "I will bring you forth, I will deliver you, I will redeem you, I will take you." I will also get you hammered. Here's looking at you, God.

**URCHATZ**: In this first of two hand-washings, we don't say the blessing. We just show all the eligible men at the Seder that there's no ring on our finger.

**KARPAS**: Next we dip parsley in salt water. The salt water reminds us of the slaves' endless tears. I wonder if they wore waterproof mascara. . . . The parsley reminds us that Passover is also the spring harvest festival. It officially kicks off the spring fling season and, ladies, the sundress is your secret weapon. Forget frogs, forget hail, forget blood—if you want a guy do what you ask, just seduce him with a cotton halter or some spaghetti straps.

**YAHATZ**: This is where that matzah tray comes into play. We uncover the three pieces of matzah and split the middle piece in two. Why do we break one piece in half? In a threesome, someone always ends up getting hurt. Also, we set that half aside to use as the *afikomen* (dessert). When no one's looking, remember to hide the afikomen so guests can look for it later in the Seder.

**MAGGID**: Have I got a story for you! Now we retell the story of our deliverance from Egypt. This disc contains some of Passover's greatest hits including: The Four Questions, The Four Sons, The Ten Plagues, Dayenu, and the story of Mo and our sprint to the sea. Here are a few highlights:

When we retell the story, we say "it's what God did for ME, when I came out of Egypt." Jews believe God not only freed our ancestors from Egypt, but all Jewish generations to come. We celebrate our own deliverance from slavery and our current freedom to be Jewish. Besides, isn't it always about you?

We read about the four sons. They represent the four types of Jews ... who you can pick up at a party. The smart son who's in law school, the wicked son who never calls, the simple son who doesn't realize you're flirting, and the son who's too young for you to date. But not too young to hook up with. Go have fun.

As we recite the ten plagues, we spill our wine out on our plates. A full cup of wine is a symbol of joy, so we empty our cups to show that we don't find joy in another person's tragedy. Unless the other person's my ex-boyfriend. Then I'm happy to hear about it. Nu, what do you know?

Be sure to brush up on your Four Questions. Traditionally they're recited by the youngest person at the table. According to the fake age you listed in your JDate profile, that would be you.

**RACHATZ**: It's the Jewish rinse, lather, repeat. Now that we've retold the Passover story, it's time for the second hand-washing, this time with the blessing.

**MOTZI MATZAH**: Jew eat yet? Me neither. I'm starving. At this point, even this plain piece of matzah we're now commanded to eat tastes great.

**MAROR**: These bitter herbs represent the hard, bitter lives of the Jewish slaves in Egypt. Whatever . . . if you think slavery makes you bitter, you should try being single.

**KOREKH**: Charoset is a chopped apple, wine, cinnamon, and nut concoction that mirrors the mortar used by our brick-building ancestors. During Korekh, we eat a bitter herbs and charoset hoagie on matzah. This flatbread sandwich, known as The Hillel, is Passover's answer to the five-dollar foot long.

**SHULHAN OREHK**: Let them eat matzah! Dinner's on—serve your guests matzah ball soup, farfel kugel, gefilte fish, and lots of other tasty Passover grub.

**TZAFUN**: Are you hiding an *afikomen* (dessert) in your pocket, or are you just happy to see me? We can't conclude the Seder until we eat the afikomen, the half piece of matzah which the hostess broke off earlier. The children—and the men who still act like them—search the house, find the matzah, and collect their prize.

**BIRKAT HAMAZON**: With the afikomen found, we recite the after-dinner blessings. They usually go something like this, "Thank God, this Seder is almost over."

**HALLEL AND ELIJAH:** We praise God and then open the door for my invisible boyfriend, Elijah. He stops by, throws back his honorary glass of wine, and leaves before anyone sees him. It's just like a man to sneak out without saying where he's going or when he'll be back.

**NIRTZAH:** We sing songs, pound on the table, chant "Next year in Jerusalem," and then collapse from exhaustion. The rabbis should change the holiday's name from Passover to Passout. After four glasses of wine, a long Seder, and a huge meal, I always pass out on my couch. Total nosh coma.

## OH MOSES, MOSES, YOU STUBBORN, SPLENDID, ADORABLE FOOL!

No, no, no, you cannot make me go. If a Seder's really not your style, then find your own way to get down with the holiday. Host a matzah brie brunch, an Iron Chef: Matzah party, or a dessert-night challenge, where friends make matzah-based sweets at home, then come together to battle for bragging rights. Or throw a *Ten Commandments* viewing party and play my favorite Passover drinking game. Take a drink anytime someone in DeMille's deliciously schmaltzy film says "Moses" and two more bonus gulps anytime someone says "'Moses, Moses." You and your friends will get drunk, drunk.

● ● ● ● ● ● ● ● ● ● ● ● ● ● ● ● ● ● ● ● ● ● ● ● ● ● ● ● ● ● ● ● ● ● ● ● ● ● ● ● ● ● ● ● ● ● ● ● ●

# THE DAYENU DIET: THE ORIGINAL LOW-CARB DIET

As you just learned, Passover's a time when Jews get together to celebrate our survival with a giant meal. So why is this holiday different from all other holidays? On all other holidays we eat bagels, on this one, matzah. Our ancestors bailed before their bread could rise, so for eight days, we avoid eating *chametz* (food that contains a forbidden grain that's been allowed to rise). Those five outlawed grains are: wheat, rye, barley, oats, and spelt. Great, it's bad enough I can't eat challah. Now I have to give up something called spelt? I eat spelt like every day, or I would if I knew what it was. And now I'll never know. At least not this week. Darn you, Passover, darn you.

## STEP AWAY FROM THE CARB

If you're *Ashkenazi* (a Jew of Eastern European descent), you'll also avoid *kitniyot* (beans, corn, rice, soy, peanuts, and legumes). Medieval European rabbis argued that kitniyot could be turned into flour and that flour into bread. If eating corn bread was okay, we'd think eating rye bread was okay, everyone would eat the wrong thing, and we'd all go down like dayenu dominoes. *Sephardic* and *Mizrahi* Jews (descending from Spain, Portugal, Israel, North Africa, or the Middle East) think the whole kitniyot thing sounds like mishegas and follow an all-you-can-eat legume policy during Passover.

## A CRUMBY HOLIDAY

Modern Jews keep kosher for Passover on a sliding scale. Some folks just say no to bread, some ban all chametz, and observant Jews only eat food that's been *hechshered* (officially marked) kosher for Passover. KFP products meet all the year-round kosher standards and on top of that don't contain, haven't touched, and weren't made in a facility with a single crumb of chametz. And your parents think you're picky about who you bring home.

Keeping kosher for Passover may sound like a pain in the tush, but it's actually easy. If you can follow Weight Watchers, Atkins, or South Beach for months, then you can stick with the Passover diet for a week. Like those diets we even have our own prepackaged Passover food that's carried by major grocery chains. At one time there weren't many processed foods produced for Passover. Outside of Streit's macaroons, Joya's jelled fruit slices, and Temp Tee cream cheese, you were on your own. Today groceries stock Passover cookies, crackers, ice cream, potato chips, microwave dinners, and frozen matzah pizzas.

Coca-Cola even produces special kosher for Passover Coke that's made with real sugar instead of corn syrup (a kitniyot). Just for us Jews, just for one week! We've come a long way, baby.

## EIGHT JARS IS ENOUGH

Maybe too far. Now that there's a glut of Passover products available, Jews buy enough food to last forty years in the desert, not eight days in the suburbs. If a product is kosher for Passover, we buy it . . . even if it's something we'd never buy during the year. If we only bought eight jars of gefilte fish and not five hard salamis, *Dayenu* (it would have been enough). If we only bought two Elite chocolate bars and not five boxes of Barton's chocolate-covered matzah, Dayenu. If we only bought two pounds of Migdal cheese and not fourteen liters of Dr. Brown's, Dayenu.

Why are we stockpiling? We're scared we'll run out of hechshered food in the middle of the holiday or crave something we decided not to throw in our cart. What if I suddenly want a dark chocolate-covered raspberry jelly ring? What if I polish off the whole can of chocolate chip macaroons by the fourth day? Oy vey iz mir! We better buy two cans. Actually, make it four.

• • • • • • • • • • • • • • • • • • • • • • • • • • • • • • • • • • • • • • •

# THE PASSOVER HOME: TWO OF EVERYTHING

Keeping Passover not only applies to food, but to everything in your home. To ensure not a speck of chametz is on anything in the kitchen, many Jews own separate dishes, utensils, and cookware just for Pesach.

Now, you don't need to run out and buy a second set of plates and pans. You can Passover-ize some of your everyday kitchenware with extreme heat and boiling water. But what kind of meshuggene girl says no to a second set of dishes? Not me. In fact, when I get married, I'm registering for four sets of dishes: year-round milk, year-round meat, Passover milk, and Passover meat. Of course, my wedding registry is a ways off, so until then, the smart Jewess like me just uses paper plates, plastic silverware, and disposable aluminum pans for Passover week. That way you're free from eating chametz and doing the dishes!

## YOU'RE NOW ENTERING A CHAMETZ-FREE ZONE

You may not be ready to turn your place into a Passover pad quite yet; but your new boyfriend just invited you for Seder, and he keeps a strict Passover home. Don't know what to expect when you're expected? Here's a little last-minute help to get you through the night:

- Don't show up to the Seder with bourbon, Scotch, or a six-pack. Beer and most hard alcohols are made from fermented grains, so an ice-cold draft is a no-no and your Scotch neat just got messy. Loophole alert: some stores stock kosher for Passover potato vodka and Slivovitz (plum brandy), in which case, feel free to drink up. L'chaim!

- Don't bake-and-bring. Even if you bake a matzah-meal cake, a rogue chametz crumb on your counter could have fallen into the batter. Oy gevalt! Now you've done it. You got peanut butter in my chocolate; you got chametz in my Pesadich. You're better off buying something hechshered from the store and using the time to fix your hair.

- When shopping at the store, read the fine print. It's not enough for food and wine to be labeled kosher; they have to be inked kosher for Passover. Other acceptable Passover food tattoos include kosher l'Pesach and the letter P with the year. I said food tattoos. Human tattoos are taboo on Jews. If you're sporting a flower on your ankle, a Japanese symbol on your wrist, or an oh-so-classy butterfly on your lower, lower back, take a lesson from the afikomen and hide it.

- If your boyfriend mentions using a feather, a candle, and a wooden spoon, don't freak out, he's not into anything kinky. During *Bedikat-Chametz* (search for chametz), Jews hunt for every last crumb of chametz, in ever last corner of their homes, using these three utensils.

- Don't feed Fido. No chametz anywhere in the house means no chametz in the dog's dish. Yup, his pup keeps Passover. His dog also has to marry another Jewish dog. It might seem like no big deal when the dogs are in heat, but it gets confusing once they start having puppies.

- If your mensch conducts a full, formal Seder, be prepared for at least a three-hour tour.

# HOW TO LOSE A GUY IN TEN PLAGUES

No matter how many times Moses tried to break up with Pharaoh, Pharaoh refused to accept that things were over. After all they'd been through together, all the years, all the memories, all those good times as slaves, he just couldn't believe that the Jews didn't want to be with him anymore. It took ten plagues for Pharaoh to finally get the message: God's just not that into you.

If you, too, are looking to dump a dreykop who will not let you go, pull a Mo and bust out one of these plagues. Rip off the Band-Aid. Give him the riding boot. Hit the road, schmuck, and don't you come back no more.

**BLOOD**: Talk to him, in detail, about your monthly visitor. Better yet, ask him to pick up a box of tampons for you when he's at the store.

**FROGS**: Tell him you knew from your first kiss that he was your frog prince. And that you expect to be treated like a total princess.

**LICE**: Start scratching your keppe like crazy and mention that your co-worker has lice . . . while you're wearing his lucky Bears hat.

**FLIES**: Bug him. Nudzh him. Hok him a chainik. Why does he spend so much time with his friends? Why doesn't he spend more money on you? What's so important about a football game? Is he really going to wear that? Why does he have to play golf? Why doesn't he send you flowers? When is he taking you ring-shopping?

**BOILS**: Cancel your facial; ignore your exfoliant; don't touch that spot treatment. Show up for a date in full-on breakout mode. I'm talking teenage acne. What? I thought all guys wanted to date a girl who looks like she's in high school.

**COWS**: Gain a few. Guys just love when their in-shape girl goes zaftig on them. Pop those kreplach, down those rugelach, eat a whole Carnegie Deli sandwich in one sitting. I was kidding. Did you seriously eat that whole thing? Yourself?

**HAIL**: Come down hard on him . . . in front of his friends. Yell, scream, and cause a scene. Public display of rejection always goes over well.

**LOCUSTS**: Just as the locust covered every inch of the Earth, you should smother every inch of his life. Be there. All the time. Every second. Even now. When he wakes up, when he lies down, when he goes to work, when he meets his friends, when he heads to the beach, when he hits the gym. Eventually he'll hit his limit.

**DARKNESS**: Insist on turning off all the lights every time you hook up.

**FIRST BORN**: Tell him you can't wait to have his first-born baby. And his second. And his third. Tick tock, tick tock.

# MATZAH LASAGNA RECIPE

This is my award-winning, well—what should have been my award-winning—matzah lasagna recipe. Where matzah meets mozzarella, this nontraditional Passover dish will quickly become a tradition in your home. It's so good that none of your guests will be able to say "no, no, no" to a second helping.

MAKES ONE 8 X 8-INCH LASAGNA

2 EGGS

16 OUNCES KOSHER FOR PASSOVER COTTAGE CHEESE

SALT TO TASTE

PEPPER TO TASTE

GARLIC POWDER TO TASTE (YES, EVEN YOUR SPICES SHOULD BE HECHSHERED K FOR P)

4 TO 6 WHOLE KOSHER FOR PASSOVER MATZAHS

1 (10.5-OUNCE) CAN KOSHER FOR PASSOVER TOMATO SAUCE WITH MUSHROOMS

8 OUNCES KOSHER FOR PASSOVER MOZZARELLA CHEESE

Preheat the oven to 350°F.

In a large bowl, beat eggs. Add cottage cheese, salt, pepper, and garlic powder.

In a separate shallow baking dish, cover the matzahs with water and let them sit until soft, but not soggy.

Spoon a little of the tomato sauce into an 8-inch square pan. Like a good miniskirt, the sauce should just barely cover your bottom.

Layer one-quarter of each of the remaining ingredients in this order: matzah, cottage cheese mixture, tomato sauce, mozzarella cheese.

Repeat layering 3 times, ending with the mozzarella.

Bake for 40 to 45 minutes.

Let stand for ten minutes before cutting, to allow the lasagna to firm up.

Serve to your guests with a mighty hand and an outstretched arm.

**TIPS:**

- Don't be intimidated by the hechsher hunt. Locating kosher for Passover ingredients is as easy as *achat, shtayim, shalosh* (one, two, three). Kosher grocery stores carry them readily and major chains like Kroger, Ralph's, Jewel, Albertson's, Shaws, Star Markets, ShopRite, Winn-Dixie, Publix, Vons, and Pavilions stock them in the weeks prior to Pesach.

- You can reheat covered leftovers for a few minutes at 325°F. But who am I kidding? You won't have leftovers—it's that good. Some might say better than Ben's.

# CHAPTER 13

# CHALLAPALOOZA
## (OTHER HOLIDAYS)

Holiday, get your holiday. Here at Jewish Holiday Central we have the right holiday for every customer. We have the largest inventory of Hebrew holidays in the world, and we won't be beat. Whatever you're into, we've got it. Save the planet? Tu B'Shevat. Like to role-play? Check out Purim. Need to diet? Yom Kippur. Looking for true love? Um, er, well . . . hmmm, I've got nothing. Zilch. Bupkes. If you're still searching for your beshert, you're on your own. I mean, of course you're on your own; if you were with someone, then you wouldn't be single. But you are single, and that's a good thing, because I'm here to propose a new Jewish holiday just for you:

Happy Yom Alone. It's about *not* bringing someone home for the holiday.

Think I've lost it? Think I'm one bagel short of a dozen? You're wrong. I'm just one short bagel (5' 2"), and I'm not ashamed to be alone. You shouldn't be either. I know, I know, everywhere you go, you're surrounded by couples—me, too. At the mall, at the movies, at the beach, I see wed people. Even Judaism is packed with twos. We've got two Torah scrolls, two Teffilin boxes, two Shabbat candles, two Shabbat challahs, two sets of dishes, two marriage ceremonies, and two tablets of the covenant. Even Noah's animals didn't have to sail off on a singles' cruise; oh no, they got to hang out on the lido deck two by two.

But if you look carefully, Judaism has plenty of single sightings, too. In fact, we've got enough to go legit with this holiday. Jewish festivals like Passover, Sukkot, and Shavuot all have a three-fold significance: spiritual, historical, and agricultural. Well, so does my Singles' Day. It's got the Hebrew holiday trifecta. On the agriculture side, the Torah tells farmers to plant only a single crop per field. On the historic front, Ruth and Naomi took a single girls' road trip through the desert. And as far as spiritual? Well, that would be the biggest singleton of all . . . God. That's right, Hear O Israel, the Lord is God, the Lord is Single. There's no Mr. and Mrs. Omnipotent, there's no Dr. and Mrs. Al Mighty, there's no his and hers tallit. Nope, God rolls by himself. He's so proud of his single status, he even engraved it into The Ten Commandments. I am your single God, you shall have no other but me. Ladies, God is a proud party of one, and you should be too. So why not celebrate Yom Alone?

Of course you can't celebrate a Jewish festival without rituals, so Yom Alone's customs would play like a holiday highlight reel. In the tradition of Passover Seders, we'll host Yom Alone dinner parties where singles can mix and mingle. In the spirit of Purim, we'll drink until everyone looks hot. And as a nod to Simchat Torah, we'll take those tipsy Jews onto the dance floor, where they'll hopefully hit it off. That way Jewish singles can get drunk, get down, and go home with someone who they know went to Hebrew School. Huh . . . maybe that's the real goal of Yom Alone, hooking up with other Heebs. I mean, it's important to have holidays that honor brave warriors like the Maccabees, and sure, those slaves deserve some respect; but single Jews deserve respect, too— and not just a little bit. We're the future of Judaism, and our religion should do everything it can to ensure we marry fellow M.O.T.s.

So let's refocus, let's think big picture. Rather than nudzh me about finding a Yom Kippur date, help me set a date for Yom Alone. Rather than hok me a chainik for flying solo to Seder, help me get signatures for my Singles' Day petition. Rather than remind me how chaloshes it is to spend Chanukah alone, help me start a new tradition: a holiday that not only celebrates hot Jewish singles, but helps pair us up.

Happy Yom Alone—it's about bringing someone Jewish home for the holiday. Or at least for the night.

...........................................................................

# LIVING THE CHAI LIFE

So maybe Yom Alone won't be widely celebrated for a while. In the meantime, there are plenty of other Jewish holidays that can help Jews hook up. I know, celebrating Big League holidays like Rosh Hashanah, Yom Kippur, and Passover can be stressful on a new relationship. So skip the pressure-cooker events and flirt your way through the farm league. Put your own spin on Simchat Torah and Sukkot. Have your own take on Tu B'Shevat and Shavuot. And get down with a little Lag B'Omer. Lag B'what? So you haven't thought about these holidays since Hebrew School; they can still pump up your social life and give your relationship a much-needed jolt. You just need to manipulate these festivals to fit your needs. Make them your own. Take back the holiday. They're a great excuse to down some drinks, see some friends, and flirt with some men.

...........................................................................

# HOLIDAY: SUKKOT

**WHAT IT IS**: The Hut Holiday
**DATE-NIGHT MISSION**: a Sukkot Slumber Party
**CATCHPHRASE**: Do you know where you are? You're in the sukkah, baby.

Who's been sleeping in my bed? No one—not that I haven't had any offers. I've just been sleeping in a hut. Observant Jews spend the week of Sukkot (Festival of

Booths) dwelling under the stars in a makeshift shed. And so should you. Think of Sukkot as the original stay-cation, but instead of staying at a hip hotel in your hometown, you're staying in a flimsy hut on your own lawn . . . hopefully with your new man. A private candlelit bungalow, moonbeams streaming in, and only each other to keep you warm. Love shack, baby, love shack.

## THE BACKGROUND

You're more into room service than roughing it, so why would you camp out? Like the rest of the Jewish holiday gang, Sukkot multitasks as a spiritual, historical, and agricultural celebration; so there are lots of reasons why we spend time in the sukkah. But since when do you need an excuse to shack up?

- Historically, our ancestors slept in huts while they wandered the desert for forty years. Great, I'm happy to honor them, but whose cockamamie idea was it to imitate the hut part? Why don't we schmy around aimlessly for a day? Or vacation in the desert for a week? I've heard Palm Springs is great this time of year. We could honor our ancestors and work on our tans. Who's in?

- On the agricultural front, Sukkot celebrates the fall harvest festival. So you can blame the sheds on the brutal commute. Rather than schlep home every night of the harvest, our ancestors put up portable huts next to their fields. It's take-your-home-to-work day.

- Spiritually, Sukkot was part of the road trip trilogy that included Passover and Shavuot. Three times a year Jews schlepped to the Temple to offer up their harvest crop. Along the way they slept in portable huts. You sure these folks are our ancestors? My relatives insist on staying at The Four Seasons. Maybe the Marriott. Worse case, the Motel 6. At least they leave the light on for you. A shack doesn't even have lights to leave on. . . .

# HOW TO PREPARE

Are you ready to hook up in the hut? Well, first you need to build one and then you need to land a man. But don't sweat the second part. If you build it, he will come. Sukkot falls five days after Yom Kippur, but Jews start hammering the first nail into their huts the minute YK ends. Why the early-bird start? If we Jews weren't delirious from hunger, we'd never agree to go Handy Andy and build a bungalow. Jews don't hang out at Home Depot. We don't watch *This Old Hut*. We don't worship a carpenter. That's the other guys.

When building your sukkah, follow the blueprints closely. The walls should be sturdy enough to withstand a breeze, but light enough to carry with you. Since our ancestors' huts were portable, our sukkot need to be temporary. Unlike Christmas lights, we actually take them down.

Raise the roof! It's the most important part of your sukkah. The sukkah walls can be made of canvas, plywood, the ugly bedspread your ex picked out—it doesn't matter; but the roof must be made from broken-off parts of growing plants. This *s'chach* (roof covering) also needs to provide more shade than sun, but let rain slip through the slats and stars shine through at night. So I'd like an organic, half-shade, half-sun, star-gazing, moonlit, partially rain-proof roof. That makes my medium, half-caf, nonfat, sugar-free mocha latte look simple. I'd hate to be in line behind God at Starbucks.

I suggest you spruce up the place before your big date night. To create a little romance, bring in paper lanterns, twinkle lights, and candles. To up the Jew factor, fulfill the commandment to bring a *lulav* (palm tree branch) and an *etrog* (lemon lookalike citrus fruit) into the hut. And to up your chances, bring in an iPod, a shag rug, and an air mattress.

Now you could gather all your supplies and build your sukkah from scratch. You could also ditch the Newman's Own sauce and make marinara from scratch, but the smart Jewess does neither. Just buy the lulav, the etrog, and an easy-to-assemble sukkah kit from your synagogue gift shop or local Judaica store. The kits include the sukkah walls, the kosher roof, and the bamboo floor mats; you just need to put them together. Don't worry, you can do it. Compared to assembling your IKEA bookshelf, constructing your sukkah-in-a-box will be a breeze.

## HOW YOU SHOULD CELEBRATE

If you're like me, you joined Girl Scouts for the cookies, not the camping. So a holiday spent holed up in a hut doesn't sound like your thing. Well, think again: shacking up in the shed can be one good time. The sukkah's like your childhood tree house, except it's not in a tree, you're not eight, and the sign now reads "All Boys Allowed." In fact, all boys encouraged. It's a mitzvah to eat (and sleep) in the hut, so invite your man over for a date night that leads to a date morning. You can wake up in the sukkah that never sleeps. Or stay up in the sukkah with a stud who never sleeps. Wow, this holiday just keeps getting better. . . .

## WHAT'S ON THE MENU?

We're commanded to eat all our meals in the sukkah, so plan a romantic dinner under the stars. Serve up seasonal apps and side dishes like roasted veggie salad, whipped sweet potatoes, or butternut squash soup. Since you're already outside, make it simple on yourself and throw steak, fish, or chicken on the grill. For dessert, I'd suggest pumpkin pie, apple strudel, or you. Show me your lulav and I'll show you my etrog. . . .

## WHAT'S ON TAP?

Looking to get sloshed in the sukkah? There are no Sukkot-specific drinks to mix up for your man, but fall harvest fruits like apples, pears, and cranberries are always hut-appropriate. So pour some autumn-inspired cocktails like stiff pear-tinis, hard apple cider, or strong Cape Cods. And of course etrogs are all the Sukkot rage, so buy a bottle of Bartenura Etrog Liqueur and serve it straight up, over ice, or in an etrog-drop martini. By the end of the night, you and your boychik will both be buzzed and need a place to crash. This hut looks comfy. . . .

# HOLIDAY: SIMCHAT TORAH

**WHAT IT IS**: We finish—and restart—reading the Torah
**DATE-NIGHT MISSION**: Rebound, baby!
**CATCHPHRASE**: We'll Be Dancing in the Streets

On Simchat Torah, we read the end and the beginning of the Torah all in one night. The holiday's instant replay teaches us that when God closes a window, he opens a door. And leaves it open, and then his mom says, "What's wrong with you, nudnik? You're letting all the cold air out!"

## THE BACKGROUND

Never mentioned in the Torah, this dance party disguised as a holiday was created by sixteenth-century rabbis. Today *Simchat Torah* (rejoicing with the Torah) is such a spirited celebration, that the dancing, drinking, and partying pours out of the synagogue and into streets. A holiday of pure joy, Simchat Torah is a total let-loose occasion. One of the most lively and exuberant nights of the year, this is where the wild Jews are.

## WHAT TO DO

Throw on your dancing shoes and get your cute tuchus to the temple. On Simchat Torah we carry the Torahs around the sanctuary in a conga line. Armed with flags, alcohol, and some serious Israeli dance moves, Jews circle the synagogue seven times. These *hakkafot* (circlings) recall the point in a Jewish wedding where the bride circles the groom seven times. No shock there; everything has to be about the happy couple under the chuppah. In fact, the person called up for the final Aliyah is called the *Chattan Torah* (groom of the Torah), and when we start over, the person called up for the first Aliyah is called the *Kallah Bereshit* (bride of Genesis). It's God's not-so-subtle way of saying, "Get out of your house, go to an ST party, and soon you'll be dancing at your own wedding." God has obviously been speaking with my mother.

## HOW TO CELEBRATE

Been down since you and your boyfriend parted like the Red Sea? Well, there's no crying in Judaism. On Simchat Torah, Jews wrap up and restart the Torah all in one night. There's no time to ask why things ended, there's no chance to mope around, there's not a moment to look back. We don't even have time for a rebound scroll. So pull a Simchat Torah and get back on the Hora. Find someone new tonight. Well, maybe not tonight. I'm not advocating a one-night stand or anything. But, seriously, good for you....

## WHAT'S ON THE MENU?

Reality bites, but it also noshes. So eat any kind of Jewish comfort food that lifts your spirits, no matter what the calorie count. Indulge in full-fat Israeli ice cream, seven-layer cake, sweet sugar kichel, chocolate chip mondelbrot, black-and-white cookies, or my favorite, chocolate-smothered nut-covered halvah. Grab a slice of chocolate babka, get in a good mood, and go bag yourself a Simchat Torah stud. Eat. Pray. Lust.

## WHAT'S ON TAP?

There's no prescribed Simchat Torah drink, so fill your flask with your choice of beverage. Some synagogues serve champagne, some serve schnapps and Slivovitz, and others mix up specialty cocktails like the Din and Tonic, the Fuzzy Pupik, and the Macher-ita (pages 161-166).

# HOLIDAY: TU B'SHEVAT

**WHAT IT IS**: Jewish Earth Day
**DATE-NIGHT MISSION**: Get him tipsy at your wine-tasting
**CATCHPHRASE**: It's so easy being green

You might remember this holiday from Hebrew school; you'd receive an oh-so-exciting certificate stating that your parents bought an Israeli tree in your honor. You would have much preferred that they bought you an Esprit outfit in your honor, but that's no reason to be bitter with Tu B'Shevat. It's one holiday you can totally use to your advantage. Feel like throwing a cocktail party? Looking to have a fun night with your new man? Looking to add benefits to an old friendship? Then host a Tu B'Shevat Seder and wine-tasting. You can commemorate the holiday, get your boy buzzed, and then bust your move.

## THE BACKGROUND

*Tu B'Shevat* (the fifteenth of Shevat) started as the Jewish tax day. Similar to America's tax day—Tu B'April—Tu B'Shevat was the day ancient farmers were required to total up their trees and tithe ten percent of their fruit to the Temple. After the Temple's destruction, Tu B'Shevat became a day for Jews worldwide to plant trees in Israel and eat Israeli produce. Today, it's expanded into a general tree-hugging holiday that would make Al Gore proud. It's not an inconvenient holiday.

## WHAT TO DO

You're off the hook. You don't need to do anything. Tu B'Shevat was all about tree-tithing; it has no religious background, so there are no official blessings, mandatory rituals, or boring synagogue services to sit through. To celebrate this New Year of Trees, most Jews just go green. We buy trees in Israel through JNF (Jewish National Fund). We plant seeds, clean up beaches, and drive a silver

Prius. We reduce our carbon footprints, care for our parks, and tend to our gardens. Not that anyone living in an apartment actually has a garden, so it's more likely that you'd tend to your one, half-dead houseplant.

# HOW TO CELEBRATE

Call your friends, dust off your decanters, and host a Tu B'Shevat Seder and wine-tasting party. The Tu B'Shevat Seder is loosely based on a Passover Seder . . . well, on all the best parts of the Passover Seder. We ditch the matzah and formal Haggadah, but keep the four glasses of wine. Yes! Started by sixteenth-century Jewish mystics, the TB Seder is the rare event that manages to bring together Kabbalists, environmentalists, and alcoholics. Oh my!

# WHAT'S ON THE MENU?

Your guests should come hungry. The Seder has four courses, each highlighting a different type of fruit. Mystics say they represent the four realms of our world. I say they represent the four types of men I date.

The first course incorporates produce like pomegranates, pineapples, and almonds. They have hard shells but edible insides and represent *Asiyah*, the physical world around us. Like a typical man, you have to work on these fruits for a while before they'll open up to you.

The second Seder course is all about *Yetzirah*, the world of emotions. You'll serve fruits like olives, dates, and apricots, which have delicious shells on the outside, but at the core? They're the pits. They represent the good-looking guys who never call the next day. Yes, I'm talking about you, Brian Stern. . . .

The third course represents *B'riyah*, the world of knowing. Serve up fruits like grapes, figs, and carobs that have delicious outsides and no pits inside. Like a real mensch, they're high-quality all the way through. If you know someone like this, I'm available for blind dates, setups, or drinks with your second-cousin Barry.

The fourth course signifies *Atzilut*, the world of spirituality. Since this world is ethereal, you can't see it, so there's no fruit to represent it. This realm is like my future husband: we're just supposed to have faith that it really exists. Enough with the faith already—show me the honey.

## WHAT'S ON TAP?

Sound the lush alarm and call your Jew friends because Tu B'Shevat sets the stage for a wild wine-tasting. We drink four different glasses of wine, one for each season. From first to fourth course, you drink white (for winter), light pink (spring), deep rose (summer), and red (fall). And I thought Joseph's coat had many colors.

Ask each of your friends to bring a bottle or two when they come over for your tree-hugging Seder. Feel free to drink kosher wines, dry wines, sweet wines, fruity wines, oaky wines, bubbly wines . . . just don't drink too much wine on Tu B'Shevat, or you'll make like a tree and fall over.

· · · · · · · · · · · · · · · · · · · · · · · · · · · · · · · · · · · · · · · · · · · · · · · ·

# HOLIDAY: LAG B'OMER

**WHAT IT IS**: A day spent outdoors
**DATE-NIGHT MISSION**: Have some fun in the sun
**CATCHPHRASE**: Shul's out for summer

Looking for an excuse to grill with your guy? Lag B'Omer's your holiday. It's like a Jewish field day filled with barbeques, bonfires, and beach volleyball games. Its origins might be a little fuzzy, but its benefits are Baccarat-clear. Lag B'Omer is the perfect pretext to throw some flip-flops on your feet, throw some hot dogs on the grill, and bond with your boy over lemonade and love. Let's get biblical, biblical. . . .

# THE BACKGROUND

Like my 21st birthday, the details behind the LBO celebration are kind of hazy. For the seven weeks between Passover and Shavuot, ancient farmers made daily *omer* (crop measurement) offerings at the Temple. This period, also called the Counting of the Omer, was a total downer—still is. Observant Jews act like they're in mourning, no haircuts, no weddings, no fun. But Lag B'Omer (the thirty-third day of omer) is a twenty-four-hour pass from the doom and gloom. On LBO, restrictions are lifted and merriment's encouraged.

Why do we get a day off? No one's quite sure. Some say it's the day a plague over Rabbi Akiva's students was lifted. Others say it's the yartzheit of Talmudic Sage Shimon bar Yochai, who wisely requested that his students mourn his death with a party. Most Jews say they aren't concerned with why we commemorate LBO, they're just happy for a random day of rejoicing. Like Bar Mitzvah bands everywhere, they're going to celebrate good times—come on!

# WHAT TO DO

Buy some SPF, a beach umbrella, and a wide-brimmed hat. Lag B'Omer celebrations are all outdoors, and the smart Jewess stays away from wrinkles. No crow's-feet for this kosher babe. Once you're protected, feel free to go full-on Gidget. Pull out your board shorts, pull your hair up in a ponytail, and go catch some Frisbees, waves, and rays.

# HOW TO CELEBRATE

There's no set religious ritual or synagogue service, so you can do anything under the sun. Invite your friends to a summer kickoff party at your place, a softball game in the park, or a big bonfire on the beach. Just grab a bikini, show off that bod, and be ready to play a little beach blanket bingo with your boyfriend.

## WHAT'S ON THE MENU?

Obviously nothing says "let's celebrate the 33rd day of counting ancient grain" like a big barbecue. So the menu is your typical boy-meets-grill story. You're looking at kosher all-beef hot dogs with a couple kosher dills on the side. Grill up a few burgers, grab some buns, and you're good to go. Since you're celebrating a Jewish holiday, you can also serve a meal with more Mediterranean flare. Toss some lamb burgers and kabobs on the 'cue and serve up sides like hummus, tabbouleh, and Israeli salad. If you're looking for something more romantic, skip the grill and pack a picnic for two. Toss a few sandwiches, some cheese and crackers, and a bottle of wine in a basket and head to an outdoor concert or a hidden grassy knoll. Nothing gets a guy frisky like a little al fresco dining.

## WHAT'S ON TAP?

Cold beer. Not because the rabbis said so, because I said so. You can't have a barbecue without ice-cold brews. In honor of the Jewish holiday, switch things up and serve some kosher hops. Most kosher markets and specialty liquor stores sell them. I recommend you pick up a few six-packs of Israel's two most popular lagers, Goldstar and Maccabee, and grab a few bottles of America's own domestic He'Brew. Throw all that beer in a big cooler, and you're looking at a real Lager B'Omer party.

If you're looking to kickstart your LBO buzz, down a bottle of Mad Dog with you friends. Not just because MD 20/20 is high proof, but because it's produced by Mogen David, the king of kosher wineries. On LBO it's a legit way to let the Jew times roll. L'chaim!

• • • • • • • • • • • • • • • • • • • • • • • • • • • • • • • • • • • • • • • • • • • •

# HOLIDAY: SHAVUOT

**WHAT IT IS**: The day God gave us the Torah
**DATE-NIGHT MISSION**: Pull an all-nighter
**CATCHPHRASE**: No Sleep in Brooklyn

Shavuot celebrates the day Moses received the Torah on Mount Sinai. To show our excitement, Jews stay up all night. You heard me, all night. I'm talking midnight until morning—so it's the perfect excuse to host the after-hours party of the year. Start chugging that Red Bull and get your rally kippah ready. We're gonna party 'til the break of dawn—Jews got it goin' on.

## THE BACKGROUND

Like Sukkot, Shavuot has agricultural, spiritual, and historical significance. I'll start with agricultural for $300, Alex.

- Shavuot marks the end of the wheat crop and the first ripening of the fruit crop. Goodbye, whole grains; hello, Jamba Jews. I'd like a Strawberry Shalom smoothie and a small Chosen People chiller. With a Talmud Boost.

- On the spiritual front, Shavuot was part of the Schlep Fest Trilogy that included Pesach and Sukkot. Three times a year Jews made pilgrimages to Jerusalem to drop their crops at the Temple. Are we there yet?

- Since the destruction of the Temple, Shavuot is best known as the Torah's book-release party. It's the day God published the first edition on Mount Sinai. A typical book signing, guests nosh on food, listen to excerpts, and pretend they've actually read the book cover to cover. Or in this case, scroll to scroll.

## WHAT TO DO

To prepare for the midnight madness, decorate your house—or tiny converted one-bedroom—with fresh flowers and foliage. The greenery's a nod to Shavuot's agricultural roots and also reminds us how the desert bloomed when we received the Torah. For us single girls, the flowers also act as a trial run for our future wedding centerpieces. I'm totally kidding, guys. Single girls don't think about what flowers we'd use in our centerpieces. Please. We think about what flowers we'd use in our bridal bouquet.

## HOW YOU SHOULD CELEBRATE

You think Shavuot's something you can skip? Well, wake up and smell the coffee. Or just stay awake after drinking coffee. From sundown to sunup, Jews worldwide are wide awake celebrating. So call your Jew crew, toss back a NoDoz, and throw a giant Shavuot study party at you place. Just be ready to make like Lionel Ritchie and go "All Night Long."

Why do we stay up past our bedtimes? Writing God a thank-you note wouldn't quite capture our gratitude for giving us the Torah—not that Jews are any good with writing thank-you notes anyways. How long did it take you to finish your Bat Mitzvah notes? Exactly. So we ditch the Crane's stationery and mount an all-night study session instead.

We're also staying up because legend says our ancestors spent three intense days getting ready to receive the Torah; but they were so tired by the time the actual day came that they overslept. So now we don't sleep at all. They slept through their meeting with the Almighty? They hit the snooze button on Mount Sinai? Those Gen A slackers . . .

## WHAT'S ON THE MENU?

On most holidays we eat brisket, but on Shavuot we only do dairy. So cook your crew a huge milchig meal, complete with kugel, blintzes, grilled cheese, cheese knish, and cheesecake. Or just order in a bunch of late-night, extra-large, four-cheese pizzas. I wonder if God delivered the Torah in twenty minutes or less. . . .

Where's the beef? Jews had never even heard of keeping kosher until God gave them the Torah. They immediately realized that none of their meat met the kosher standards, and they frantically threw it out, hoping God wouldn't notice.

As if the Almighty didn't know what they ate yesterday. Hello, McFly ... he's the Almighty.

## WHAT'S ON TAP?

You're supposed to serve your Shavuot guests the seven species of the First Fruits (grapes, barley, wheat, pomegranates, figs, olives, and dates). I suggest you pour them. Stock your bar with wine (grapes), Scotch (barley), hefeweizen (wheat), Pomaritas (pomegranates), whiskey fig fizzes (figs), and dirty martinis (olives). Then your friends can drunkenly hook up, exchange digits, and make plans for Friday night (dates).

# SHAVUOT BLINTZ SOUFFLE

Shavuot is all about milchig mania. Dairy, dairy everywhere and not a meat to eat. If you want to snaz up your standard bagel and cream cheese spread, bust out this blintz dish. This simple soufflé is quick to impress, but easy to make. The secret is to start with frozen blintzes. Why make your own when you can buy someone else's?

**SERVES 6**

12 KOSHER CHEESE BLINTZES, DEFROSTED

½ CUP MARGARINE

4 EGGS, WELL-BEATEN

1½ CUPS SOUR CREAM

¼ CUP SUGAR

½ TEASPOON SALT

2 TEASPOONS VANILLA

1 TEASPOON ORANGE JUICE (OPTIONAL)

Preheat the oven to 350°F.

Melt margarine and pour into a 9 x 11-inch pan.

In a single layer, place defrosted blintzes over the melted margarine.

Pour yourself a glass a wine. This has nothing to do with the recipe, but since you're already in the kitchen . . .

In a large bowl, mix the eggs, sour cream, sugar, salt, vanilla, and juice.

Pour the egg mixture over the blintzes.

Bake for 45 minutes. Take a shower, straighten your hair, and do your makeup while it cooks. By the time the soufflé is ready, so are you.

**TIPS:**

- Serve quickly, before the soufflé falls. . . . If your soufflé does fall, don't get all ferklempt. It'll still taste great.
- Kosher blintzes can be found in the freezer aisle at all kosher grocery stores and most major supermarkets.
- To help your soufflé rise, keep the oven door closed. It won't be the first time you've hung a Do Not Disturb sign on the door. . . .

# HEEBONICS GLOSSARY

**ABBA**: father
**AFIKOMEN**: a dessert; the broken piece of matzah hidden during Seder
**ALEVAI**: "it should only happen"
**ALIYAH**: to go up; to be called up to the Torah
**ALTER KOCKER**: "old crap," old fart, senior citizen
**ASHKENAZI**: Jews of Eastern and Central European descent
**AVOT**: Judaism's patriarchs: Abraham, Isaac, and Jacob
**BADECKEN**: to cover up; veiling ceremony
**BALABUSTA**: an expert housewife
**BAR/BAT MITZVAH**: Son/Daughter of Commandment
**BET DIN**: a religious court of three Jewish adults
**BEIT K'NESSET**: House of Gathering
**BEIT MIDRASH**: House of Study
**BEIT TEFILAH**: House of Prayer
**BENTSCH**: to bless; reciting the grace after meals
**BESHERT**: meant to be, fated, soul mate
**BIMAH**: a raised sanctuary platform
**BISSEL**: a small amount
**BOYCHIK**: boy (affectionate)
**BRIS/BRIT MILAH**: covenant of circumcision
**B'SAMIN**: spices
**BUBBE**: grandmother
**BUBBE MAISEH**: "grandmothers's story"; made-up story
**BUBELEH**: "little grandmother"; darling (affectionate)
**BUPKES**: "beans"; nothing or insultingly small amount
**CHAI**: life; design often reproduced in jewelry and Judaica; numerical value of the word *chai* is 18, which is why it's considered a lucky number
**CHAIM YANKEL**: Joe Schmo, country bumpkin
**CHALOSHES**: revolting, disgusting
**CHAMETZ**: leavened grains forbidden during Passover
**CHANUKIAH**: Chanukah menorah
**CHATTAN**: groom
**CHAVURAH**: fellowship
**CHAZZER**: pig; stingy, greedy
**CHAZZERAI**: trash, junk
**CHUPPAH**: wedding canopy
**CHUTZPAH**: gall, nerve
**COCKAMAMIE**: ridiculous

**DAVEN**: to pray
**DREK**: excrement; garbage
**DREYKOP**: "turned head"; confused or confusing person
**EREV**: eve
**ESS**: to eat
**FAPUTZED**: dressed up
**FARBRENT**: burnt
**FARBRISSENER**: bitter person
**FARKAKTE**: crapped up, messed up, screwed up
**FARMISHT**: mixed up, shook up
**FARSHIKKERT**: drunk
**FARSHTINKER**: stinking
**FEH**: expression of disgust
**FERKLEMPT**: choked up
**FLEIGEL**: wing
**FLEISHIG**: meat
**FORSHPEIZ**: appetizer
**FRESS**: to eat heartily
**FRUM**: observant Jew
**FUTZ**: to fiddle with
**GELT**: money
**GEMILUT CHASADIM**: acts of lovingkindness
**GORNISHT**: nothing
**GOY**: non-Jew
**GOYISHER KOP**: "Gentile head"; non-Jewish thinking
**GRAGGOR**: Purim noisemaker
**HAGGADAH**: "telling"; book of the Passover story
**HAIMESH**: homey
**HALACHA**: Jewish law
**HAMOTZI**: blessing over bread
**HANDEL**: to bargain
**HAVDALAH**: separation, Shabbat's closing ceremony
**HECHSHER**: kosher seal of approval
**HOK A CHAINIK**: "to strike a teapot"; relentless nagging
**HORA**: a traditional circle dance
**IMA**: mother
**IMAHOT**: Judaism's matriarchs: Sarah, Rebecca, Rachel, and Leah
**KABBALAT SHABBAT**: welcome the Sabbath
**KADDISH**: a prayer glorifying God, often recited during mourning
**KALLAH**: bride
**KAPUT**: finished

**KASHER**: to make kosher
**KEPPE**: head
**KETUBAH**: marriage contract
**KIBBITZ**: to meddle; to tease, joke around; to make small talk
**KIDDUSH**: sanctification; blessing over wine
**KIDDUSHIN**: betrothal
**KINE-AHORA**: said to ward off the evil eye
**KIPPAH**: skullcap
**KISHKE**: intestine; guts; a stuffed side dish
**KITNIYOT**: beans, corn, rice, soy, peanuts, and legumes
**KITTEL**: white ceremonial robe
**KOSHER**: fit, proper; in accordance to Jewish dietary laws
**KRIAH**: tearing of cloth during mourning period
**KVELL**: to beam with pride
**KVETCH**: "to press"; to complain
**LADINO**: Spanish–Hebrew language spoken by Sephardim
**LATKE**: potato pancake
**L'CHAIM**: to life
**LECK**: a taste
**LOCH IN KOP**: a hole in the head
**LOKSHEN**: noodles
**MA'ARIV**: evening service
**MACHER**: big shot
**MATZAH**: unleavened bread
**MAVEN**: expert
**MAZEL TOV**: congrats on your recent good luck
**MECHITZA**: partition, found in Orthodox synagogues
**MEGILLAH**: scroll; the Purim story; a long story
**MELACHOT**: acts of creating forbidden on Shabbat
**MENORAH**: candelabra
**MENSCH**: literally "person"; an honorable, thoughtful, unselfish, admirable person
**MESHUGGENE**: crazy
**MIESKEIT**: ugly girl
**MIKVAH**: ritual bath
**MILCHIG**: dairy
**MINCHA**: afternoon service
**MINYAN**: quorum of ten Jewish adults
**MISHEGAS**: craziness
**MISHPACHA**: family
**MITZVAH**: commandment; good deed
**MOHEL**: person who performs a bris

**MONDLEN**: soup nuts, a ball-shaped cracker
**M.O.T.**: "Member of the Tribe"; Jewish person
**MUKTZA**: tools used for work
**MUSAF**: additional service
**NACHES**: joy
**NEBBISH**: a loser
**NER TAMID**: eternal light
**NETILAT YADAYIM**: washing of the hands
**NISSUIN**: nuptials
**N.J.B.**: nice Jewish boy
**NO-GOODNIK**: someone who's no good
**NOSH**: snack
**NOSHERAI**: snack food
**NU**: "so . . ."
**NUCHSCHLEPER**: person who schleps along, a hanger-on
**NUDNIK**: a pest
**NUDZH**: to pester
**OMER**: ancient crop measurement
**ONEG SHABBAT**: joy of Sabbath; post-Shabbat service reception
**ONGEPOTCHKET**: thrown together; excessively decorated
**OY**: oh!
**OY GEVALT**: literally "oh help"; negative astonishment
**OY VEY**: oh no!
**OY VEY IZ MIR**: oh woe is me!
**PAREVE**: neutral
**PE'OT**: literally "corners"; side curls
**PISHER**: bed wetter; inexperienced person
**PLOTZ**: burst
**POTCHKEH**: fuss
**POULKE**: thigh
**PUPIK**: navel
**PUSHKE**: little container
**RABBI/RAV**: teacher; ordained leader
**RACHMONES**: compassion, pity
**SCHLEMIEL**: a fool
**SCHLEP**: to drag or lug (an object or yourself)
**SCHLIMAZEL**: an unlucky person
**SCHLOCK**: cheaply made, shoddy thing
**SCHMALTZ**: chicken fat; grease
**SCHMALTZY**: greasy; overly sentimental
**SCHMATTE**: rag

**SCHMEKEL**: a penis
**SCHMENDRIK**: a non-mensch; a jerk
**SCHMOOZE**: to chat, to network, to have a heart to heart
**SCHMUCK**: literally a penis; a jerk
**SCHMY**: meander
**SCHTICK**: a routine or bit
**SCHMUTZIDIK**: dirty
**SCHNOOK**: a passive dope
**SCHNORRER**: a mooch, cheapskate
**SCHNOZ**: nose
**SCHTUP**: to push; to have sex
**SCHVITZ**: sweat
**SEDER**: order; the ritual Passover meal
**SEPHARDIC**: Jews who descend from Spain, Portugal, Israel, North Africa, and the Middle East
**SEUDAT HAVRA'AH**: meal of condolence
**SEUDAT MITZVAH**: a commanded post-mitzvah meal
**SHABBAT**: rest; Sabbath
**SHACHARIT**: morning service
**SHADCHAN**: matchmaker
**SHALOM**: peace; hello; goodbye
**SHAMAS**: worker; helper candle
**SHANDA**: shame
**SHAYNA MAIDEL**: pretty girl
**SHAYNA PUNIM**: pretty face
**SHEITEL**: wig
**SHEKEL**: a coin currency
**SHEKET BEVAKASHA**: quiet, please
**SHEMA**: declaration of one God
**SHEVA BRACHOT**: seven marriage blessings
**SHIDDUCH**: match
**SHIKSA**: non-Jewish girl
**SHIVA**: literally seven; mourning period
**SHMEAR**: spread
**SHMEGEGGE**: a drip
**SHOFAR**: ram's horn blown on High Holidays
**SHOMER SHABBOS**: Shabbat observant
**SHPILKES**: pins and needles
**SHPRITZ**: spray
**SHUL**: Yiddish for "synagogue", from the word meaning "school"
**SIDDUR**: prayer book

**SIMCHA**: happy occasion

**SPIEL**: a play; a long-winded speech or story

**SUFGANIYOT**: donuts

**SUKKAH**: temporary hut erected for Sukkot

**SVELTE**: slender

**SYNAGOGUE**: house of worship

**TALLIT/TALLIS**: prayer shawl, interchangeably spelled and pronounced as "tallit" and "tallis"

**TALMUD**: large compilation of rabbis' commentaries

**TASHLICH**: cast away; Rosh Hashanah service

**TCHOTCKE**: trinket

**TEFILAH**: prayer

**TEFILLEN**: prayer boxes

**TEMPLE**: (with a capital T), refers to the ancient Temple in Jerusalem

**TESHUVA**: literally to return; to repent

**TIKKUN OLAM**: heal the world

**TORAH**: five books of Moses

**TRAYF**: nonkosher

**TSOURIS**: trouble, problems

**TUCHUS**: rear end

**TZEDAKAH**: righteous giving

**TZITZIT**: fringes

**TZNIUT**: modesty

**VIDDUI**: confessional prayer

**YAD**: literally "hand"; the pointer used while reading the Torah

**YARMULKE**: skullcap

**YARTZHEIT**: literally "year's time"; anniversary of a death

**YENTA**: a gossip or chatterbox

**YICHUD**: post-wedding seclusion

**YIZKOR**: memorial service

**YONTIF**: holiday

**ZAFTIG**: juicy, plump

**ZAYDE**: grandfather

**ZHLUB**: slob, graceless person

# ACKNOWLEDGMENTS

**A trendy yenta like me doesn't get her first book published without the help of others. So a giant *toda raba* (thank you) to:**

My parents, Maer and Bonnie Davis, who have always supported my dreams and encouraged me to go after them. Thank you for creating a warm, fun, loving, Jewish home for our family and for passing along the recipes and traditions that make our holidays together so special. I guess now's the time to also publicly thank you for schlepping me to and from Hebrew School for all those years.

My brothers, Adam, Jordan, and Eddie Davis, for being true mensches.

My editor, Kristen Green Wiewora, for her invaluable insight, spot-on suggestions, and endless enthusiasm. You're a real maven when it comes to this book stuff.

The rest of the talented team at Running Press—including designer Joshua McDonnell, who gave this book its fabulous look, publicist Nicole DeJackmo, and proofreader Cathy East.

The literary machers at Dystel & Goderich—especially my agent, Lauren Abramo, for her patient guidance, great advice, and wholehearted support. And Adina Kahn, for believing in my proposal from the start.

Everyone at *The Jewish Journal of Greater Los Angeles*—I'm so proud to be a part of such a great paper. Thank you for helping me to combine my three passions in life: writing, Judaism, and kvetching about Jewish men.

Rabbi Daniel Greyber, for his time, friendship, and keen proofreading skills.

All the nuchschlepers, schlemiels, and schmucks I've dated, for giving me such great writing material.

And Ross, for his lovingkindness.